Pregnancy
Sucks

2nd Edition

Pregnancy Sucks

2nd Edition

What to Do When Your Miracle Makes You *Both* Miserable

Joanne Kimes,
author of *Pregnancy Sucks*
and Jeff Kimes

Avon, Massachusetts

Published by
Adams Media, a division of F+W Media, Inc.
57 Littlefield Street, Avon, MA 02322. U.S.A.
www.adamsmedia.com

ISBN 10: 1-4405-2678-8
ISBN 13: 978-1-4405-2678-7
eISBN 10: 1-4405-2799-7
eISBN 13: 978-1-4405-2799-9

Printed in the United States of America.

10 9 8 7 6 5 4 3 2 1

Library of Congress Cataloging-in-Publication Data
is available from the publisher.

This publication is designed to provide accurate and authoritative information with regard to the subject matter covered. It is sold with the understanding that the publisher is not engaged in rendering legal, accounting, or other professional advice. If legal advice or other expert assistance is required, the services of a competent professional person should be sought.

—From a *Declaration of Principles* jointly adopted by a Committee of the American Bar Association and a Committee of Publishers and Associations

Many of the designations used by manufacturers and sellers to distinguish their product are claimed as trademarks. Where those designations appear in this book and Adams Media was aware of a trademark claim, the designations have been printed with initial capital letters.

This book is intended as general information only, and should not be used to diagnose or treat any health condition. In light of the complex, individual, and specific nature of health problems, this book is not intended to replace professional medical advice. The ideas, procedures, and suggestions in this book are intended to supplement, not replace, the advice of a trained medical professional. Consult your physician before adopting any of the suggestions in this book, as well as about any condition that may require diagnosis or medical attention. The author and publisher disclaim any liability arising directly or indirectly from the use of this book.

This book is available at quantity discounts for bulk purchases.
For information, please call
1-800-289-0963.

dedication
To my husband, Jeff

Thank you for sticking by me throughout my troublesome pregnancy, my oversensitive nature, and my occasional undercooked chicken. I love you with all my heart.

contents

Chapter 8

Chapter 9

acknowledgments

First and foremost, I wish to thank my daughter, Emily, without whom this book would never have been written. Even though she made my life difficult while growing inside of me, once she came out, she made it complete.

My eternal gratitude to my editor, Kate Epstein, and all the kind people at Adams Media, for giving me the opportunity to write another book. Not only did this allow for another wish fulfilled, it also provided me the luxury of being a stay-at-home mom that much longer.

To my sister, Laurie, who performed generous babysitting duty as my deadline approached. All of those long treasure hunts and macaroni-and-cheese lunches are greatly appreciated.

A big thank-you to the numerous men who shared their innermost feelings about pregnancy with me—Robert Schroer, Matthew Greenberg, Jay O'Donnel, Tom Whyte, Jesse Albert, David Stokes, Brian Jones, Ted Bonnitt, Chris Jackson, and Paul Kaplan. And to the many others who shared their feelings but made me swear on my life that I would never use their real names.

And finally, thank you to my husband, Jeff, for helping to create not only this book, but the baby who inspired it.

introduction

by Joanne Kimes

When I found out that I was pregnant I was the happiest woman alive. After years of hoping, my dream had finally come true. But what I thought would be nine months of bliss turned into nine months of *blecch*. And worse yet, I couldn't utter a single complaint to my friends and family for fear of being perceived as the worst mother-to-be in the world. For complaining when you're pregnant is looked upon by mankind as unwomanly and downright sinful. Instead of keeping quiet like a good little pregnant girl, I wrote a book about what a difficult time reproducing can be and called it *Pregnancy Sucks*.

Several months after the book was finished I got a call from Kate, my editor. "We were thinking that you should write a companion book for *Pregnancy Sucks*," said Kate. "It would be a book from a man's point of view about all the unpleasant aspects that fathers-to-be have to go through as well." I thought about it for a second and said, "Yeah, that sounds like a great idea!" Truth be told, it wasn't so much that I thought the idea was so hot, but I sure wasn't going to pass up a book deal when one was thrown my way. But after Kate hung up I wondered how I could ever write such a book. How much did pregnancy really suck for men anyway? Sure, they have to live with a cranky wife and have less sex, but does it really suck? I didn't think so.

I turned to my husband, Jeff, and told him what Kate had proposed. I told him that a book that lists all the ways pregnancy sucked for men would be shorter than one that listed the Cubs' winning seasons. But then Jeff did something truly surprising. He didn't laugh. (That's not really the surprising part, because Jeff doesn't always get my sense of humor. This is a source of frustration for me, but he knows how to fix things around the house so I forgive him.)

What was surprising about that moment was the serious look on his face. "What is it?" I asked in the loving, caring way that I always do. "Is there something you didn't tell me when I was pregnant? Was it really all that hard for you?" Then, after years of keeping quiet, Jeff finally admitted the truth. He poured his heart out and told me about the dozens of reasons why he too found the reproductive process so difficult to handle. The truth poured out of him with the force of Niagara Falls. It was as if the pregnancy floodgate had finally been lifted.

I asked Jeff why he had never mentioned this to me when I was pregnant, and he gave me two very good reasons. The first one was, just like with an expectant woman, it was socially incorrect for future fathers to complain about their wives' pregnancy. If he did, he would be seen as the loser of all husbands and not worthy of the blessing that had been bestowed upon him. His second reason was simpler: pure survival instinct. I admit that when I was pregnant, I had a mood swing or two. So Jeff did what every other father-to-be does: He kept his mouth shut.

Because of Jeff's honesty, I decided that Kate was right. This book should be written. It's a story that must be told so that the truth can finally be revealed. Pregnancy does suck for men as well. But I knew that I couldn't write this book alone. Doing so would go against my cardinal rule of writing: Write what you know. And I know one thing for sure: I am not a man who has lived with a pregnant woman.

Just then a light bulb went on above my head. (It was only Jeff fixing the overhead light fixture—see, he really is quite handy to have around—but it still gave me the inspiration that I needed.) Jeff should help me write the book! He's the one who can provide the male perspective that it so desperately needs. He's the one who can supply the difficult topics that I'll need to focus on. And by far the most important thing, he can give it a voice. We would work together on the book, and it would be written from Jeff's perspective. We both know that after hearing your wife rant and rave all day, the last thing you want is to listen to another woman telling you what you need to know.

So Jeff and I worked together and designed *Pregnancy Sucks for Men* to be the quintessential guide for the father-to-be. It's a book that's geared toward the interests of men and focuses on the problems and issues that they'll face during the months ahead. It offers numerous ways in which they can help their wives with their uncomfortable pregnancy ailments. And it also gives expectant fathers the woman's perspective on some hot topics so that they can dodge the inevitable bullets that hormones and mood swings can fire off. And, for no extra cost, you'll also receive a monthly update of your baby's development so that you'll know what he's been up to while he causes such havoc.

It seems that every few years the "rules" of pregnancy get tweaked. New products are created. New trends set in motion. But this brand-spanking-new second edition of *Pregnancy Sucks for Men* is chock full of the latest and greatest pregnancy and birthing advice. With this book in hand, you can keep up to date in your role of daddy-to-be. I hope it gives you the tools you'll need to survive these next nine months. I hope it enlightens you about the changes that are taking place in you, your wife, and your child. And I hope that by learning a few tricks, you can take away some of your wife's discomfort and in turn make her happy. Because that, my friend, is what pregnancy for men is really all about.

introduction

by Jeff Kimes

When my wife asked me to help her write this book, I was hesitant. To be honest, I'm not much of a writer. (I'm not much of a reader either, unless you count the Sunday sports page.) But I did have a thing or two to say about living with an expectant woman.

When Joanne was pregnant with our daughter, Emily, I had some rough times to deal with, but all in all, I think I did a pretty good job of keeping her happy. I doted on her every need. I rubbed her achy feet until I had achy hands. And I told her that she hardly even looked pregnant even though she looked like she was put through that FatBooth phone app.

But even with all of my tender loving care, my wife saw me as a father-to-be failure. For I had committed the worst offense a man living with a pregnant wife can do: I didn't read a pregnancy book. For some reason, my wife saw this as the number-one most important thing that I could do to prove my love for my wife and my unborn child. And even with my limited knowledge of the female species, I would bet that your wife has this same odd belief system. That's why, even more important than the things you'll learn in this book, you will be making her happy simply by picking it up and reading it.

I, for one, can understand how hard you've tried to read pregnancy books in the past. You've picked up one of the dozen or so books that are stacked high on your wife's night-stand and glanced through it. You've flipped through page after page of technical mumbo-jumbo and scary prenatal health risks for both your child and your wife, and thrown the book down in disgust. And then came that overwhelm-ing feeling of failure.

Believe me, I know all about this problem. I too had a nightstand full of pregnancy books and would have given anything if I could have gotten through just one of them, for I knew how much my wife wanted me to. I could have stuck a porn magazine inside the pages for all she'd care. She'd still give me credit for trying. But I couldn't do it. And to this day, years after our daughter was born, she still resents me for it. Believe me, there are so many reasons that your wife will resent you during these next nine months that you don't want to piss her off so early on in the reproductive process.

I understand how you feel. You don't have a uterus and don't want to read a book that celebrates them. But who knows, maybe by reading this book you can help soothe some of your wife's pregnancy aches and pains. You might have a greater understanding about the miraculous process that's taking place inside your wife's belly. You might even have a greater insight to your wife's feelings (yeah, like that'll ever happen). And, for whatever reason, if you still can't manage to read this book, just stick a porn magazine inside of it and pretend to. Maybe she'll give you credit for trying, too.

prelude

The Art of Conception

No doubt the vast majority of the men who are reading this book have already knocked up their wives. But there may be a handful of you out there who are still trying to conceive. Or maybe you had a pregnancy before and suffered a miscarriage, as my wife and I did, and are now back in the reproductive saddle once again. Either way, I hope to offer the advice, sympathy, and compassion you'll need when tackling the sometimes nearly impossible feat of getting that sperm to penetrate that egg. Besides, even if you are pregnant, maybe you'll get a few chuckles looking back at the ordeals you faced in order to get a good tax write-off.

You've likely realized by now that conception may not happen right way. More often these days, women have chosen to wait until their careers are established before starting a family. While all of those years have plumped up her 401(k), it's shriveled up her eggs like microscopic raisins. Because of this, Mother Nature often needs help with conception that only a trip to the local drugstore can provide.

Your wife has probably read up on the various methods to conceive. In fact, you may be trying out these different techniques to speed the process along. But no matter which method you choose, there is one thing that you can count on for sure. Your sex life is going to change. Say goodbye to those days of spontaneous sex. From now on you can expect to abstain from sex for several days or even weeks so that your sperm count has a chance to increase. Then, you can only have intercourse when your wife is ovulating, and she'll expect you to perform on cue. If you can't get it up your wife will put you out, for she knows that if the timing isn't just right, she'll have to endure another month of being slapped in the face by the hands of her biological clock.

Not Tonight Honey, Your Basal Thermometer Is Giving Me a Headache

You've all heard the saying that there's no such thing as bad sex, but any man who is trying to conceive will tell you otherwise. Before trying to conceive, your wife might not have been in the mood for sex because of a headache (or at least that's what she told you); now, the entire process of trying to create a baby can give you one big headache.

Maybe your headache is due to the fact that you've had to undergo so many lifestyle changes. In order for you to be at your most fertile best, you're forbidden from taking hot showers, relaxing in Jacuzzis, or consuming even the tiniest drop of caffeine or alcohol. Your snug and comfy briefs have been replaced by roomy boxers that have the uncomfortable habit of letting the mule out of the barn door.

Maybe you have a headache because your wife has denied your manly needs for so long. She knows far too well that abstinence plays an important part in beefing up your sperm count. Those important tadpoles are now like little Thanksgiving turkeys that have to plump up for the big day. Sure, you may be so frustrated that you're tempted to take matters into your own hand, but don't even think about it. If your wife sees you wiping those millions of potential offspring away onto a Kleenex, there'll be hell to pay.

Maybe your head hurts because your formerly sane wife has become completely obsessed with reproducing. I know that my wife searched for her ovulation day with the intensity of an Amber Alert. Instead of spending her time doting on my every need, she spent her days taking her temperature, peeing on ovulation predictor sticks, and searching for her "egg-white" (trust me, if you don't know what that term means, consider yourself lucky).

Your headache could also be brought on because of the kind of sex that you're now forced to have. Gone is the tenderness that was once shared by husband and wife. Making love has been reduced to "stick it in and get it over with" before your wife's window of conception slams shut on your penis. If you're using an ovulation predictor kit, you may have had to endure this pressure-cooker sex for three nights in a row (if you're over forty, that may involve more labor than her delivery). After you perform your stud service, all your wife will want to do is to lie on her back with her legs in the air like a dead cockroach. You never thought it was possible, but you actually miss the days when you were forced to cuddle.

Maybe your head is throbbing because you're trying for a child of a particular sex. Believe it or not, there are numerous books that teach you the various sexual techniques that could influence your baby's chances of becoming either a boy or a girl. It seems that "boy" sperms are better swimmers but there are less of them around. "Girls" are more plentiful, but don't seem to like getting their hair wet in the gene pool. The theory is that if you abstain for a certain amount of time and have sex in a certain position, it could affect the outcome of the baby's gender.

Yes, conception sex can definitely give you one big pain in the head. But I want to let you in on a little secret that may change the way you think about it: Even if conception sex is a disappointment, even if it doesn't have the excitement and spontaneity it did in the past, you should savor every moment of it. Because if your wife conceives, it just may be the last sex that you're going to have for a very long time.

If I'm So Good in Bed, Why Is My Aim So Bad?

It's downright frustrating. You've been trying to conceive for months, maybe even years, and all your hard work has been unsuccessful. Your wife cries at the end of every month. Your parents and in-laws continue to hound you for grandchildren. Even that monthly egg is pissed off because it's lost its big chance to grow up to be president. And for some reason, it's you that feels the brunt of the guilt. For even though it takes two to conceive, society thinks it's the man's job to impregnate the woman.

So what's the problem here anyway? Men are supposed to be naturally good with their aim. They're the hunters. They've had millions of years to perfect their skill slaying woolly mammoths. That's why men are drawn to sports. They like to throw a baseball over a plate, and kick a football between two posts. They hit golf balls into tiny holes and slam tennis balls directly into their opponent's court. So what's wrong with your aiming skills? Were your ancestors some kind of prehistoric vegans?

What would really be nice is if there were some kind of target practice available to hone your reproduction skills. Sort of like a driving range for ejaculation. A place where a man could go with his equipment in hand and practice his stroke. Afterward he'd be given a scorecard ranking his distance and speed so he could determine where his errors lie. Maybe he isn't driving his shot far enough down the fairway. Maybe his club is crooked, so he's hooking to the right.

I know you're frustrated that it's taking so long for you to sink one into the basket. You feel like a sexual wimp as you watch other fathers push their strollers down the street. It seems that in the game of conception, you're the last one to be picked for the team. But chances are, if you keep practicing your aim, you're sure to make a slam dunk.

How to Make Love to a Cup

After a few months of unsuccessful attempts to conceive, it's time to call in the big guns: the fertility clinic. These modern facilities make use of the latest technology and the sleekest professional decorators. And why shouldn't they? The first thing that you'll notice about these places is that they are frightfully expensive. Your doctor is basically giving you a baby in exchange for a 50-inch 3-D plasma television.

At your first appointment, the doctor will need to figure out where the fault lies. Although you both tell each other that it doesn't matter whose fault it is (and it really shouldn't), deep down, it does. It's not that you want there to be anything wrong with your wife, but I guarantee that you'll breathe a big sigh of relief if your sperm count comes back in the "ha ha, it's not my problem" range.

Unfortunately, no matter who has the faulty wiring, you'll still be faced with the challenge of having to be intimate with a cup. For some of you this task may not be much of a problem. You've made love to less memorable receptacles after a college kegger. In fact, some of you may even enjoy the process, as it may very well be the only time in your married life that your wife will actually encourage you to watch porn. She may even root you on and tell you to go for the girl-on-girl stuff that she knows you like so well.

While at the fertility clinic, you'll be brought into a room and left alone to seek inspiration. You'll be like a kid in an X-rated candy shop sampling all the tasty morsels. There will be shelves upon shelves full of porn magazines with hot centerfolds. You'll have at your disposal dozens of erotic videos that may have not been given the critical thumbs-up, but do manage to raise a different part of your anatomy.

But like every other good thing in life, having sex with a cup has its downside. To begin with, it may freak you out a little knowing what's been going on in that room before you got there. The floors feel sticky and you might worry that you're sitting in a wet spot. It can give anyone a good case of the heebie-jeebies. At times, going in for your monthly deposit can be downright upsetting. Many guys develop a fondness for a certain porn star because of the intimate relationship they've shared, and it's a letdown to find that she's not there for them when they need her. It seems that part of the high price of fertility treatments goes toward replacing a large quantity of material that somehow gets "lost."

And what if it takes you a long time to satisfy the cup? Going slow can be great when there's an actual woman involved, but not so much when you're alone with a plastic drinking container. What if your volume is low and your nurse is hot? I know of many a man who was tempted to spit into the cup in order to pump up the volume. Worse still, what if you fail to provide a sample at all? If you can't do your manly duty with a room full of porn, there's really no hope for you at all. You'll hand your empty cup to the hot nurse, and she'll give you the same unsatisfied look that your wife does when another pregnancy test stick comes up negative. Everywhere you turn, there's pressure.

I know that it can be hard seducing a cup month after month. Actually, I don't really know, but I'm trying to appear empathetic. It only took a few months for us to become pregnant, but to tell the truth, I'm a bit jealous of anyone who has to go to a fertility clinic. I could go for a little sanctioned girl-on-girl stuff myself.

Whose Wife Is This Anyway?

If you think that jerking off in a cup is hard, take a look at what your wife has to endure in order for her to go forth and multiply. If the problem lies with her equipment, she'll have to undergo treatments that are far more invasive and painful than what you had to go through. Whether she has to endure artificial insemination, in vitro fertilization, or simply renew her eggs, which have been stewing in their own juices for far too long, she may have to subject herself to daily injections of hormones for several days to several weeks before she ovulates.

For the price of a small island, her doctor will give her a kit that contains the needles, syringes, and vials she'll need to shoot up for the month. These injections are going to need to be given in either your wife's stomach or her ass, and, unless she's double-jointed (in which case, congratulations), she may find this difficult. She may have trouble reaching the target area or getting the needle in at just the right angle. Or, unless she's been an intravenous drug user in the past, she may be understandably hesitant to stick herself with a needle. Because of this, she's going to turn to you for help.

You'll probably be a bit nervous at first, as you don't want to hurt her. If you want, you can practice giving injections to an orange first. If the orange doesn't run away screaming in pain, you're good to go.

The first few injections may take some time, but pretty soon you'll become as good as any Beverly Hills dermatologist dispensing Botox. Within no time you'll be able to inject her with one hand and do the crossword puzzle with the other. Who knows—after all is said and done, it may even be fun. Sure, you may not be a doctor, or even play one on TV, but you can play one near the TV in your own home.

But the injections aren't the worst part of the treatment. That will happen next. Not long after being given her shot, your wife will become a crazed lunatic. She'll experience the anger and wrath of PMS, the likes of which you've never seen before. Although the doctor has told you that the shots contain chemicals to increase the quality of her egg production, you're not sure that you believe him. After seeing the effects these drugs have on your wife, you're convinced that they contain the same chemicals that turned Bruce Banner into the Incredible Hulk.

After a while it may all seem like too much to take. You may be tempted to water down her medication like she does your gin. Or you can make another move altogether . . . get out of the house! Fake a business trip or a family emergency. God knows she's faked it with you from time to time, so turnabout is fair play. I know that making up lies to avoid your loved one isn't the best thing to do, but it will give you practice for the days ahead. Once those pregnancy hormones set in, they set in hard. And somehow they not only last through the pregnancy, childbirth, and nursing, but they don't go away until . . . well, I'll have to get back to you on that one.

Bull's-Eye!

You thought the day would never come. Your wife finally conceived! For some of you, this miracle of nature took years of struggle and thousands of dollars in fertility treatments. For others, all that was required was a glass of wine and a night of boring reruns. But finally, after months or even years of trying, your wife finally utters the words you've been longing to hear: "We can have spontaneous sex again!" Actually, she tells you that she's pregnant, but you only hear what you want to hear. You're shocked, elated, and proud. You finally did what you were put on this earth to do: Get somebody knocked up!

But although the powers that be have dealt you a wonderful hand, you should play your next card very carefully.

You need to realize that after your wife tells you the good news, the next words that come from your mouth will be some of the most important words that you will ever say. They'll be rehashed at family get-togethers and repeated to every one of her girlfriends in the utmost detail. Because of this, the next words that spew from your lips will need to reflect both how ecstatic you are about the baby, and how much you love your wife. Any other type of response—like "Are you sure it's mine?" or "Good, now my kid that I never told you about will have a sibling"—is strictly forbidden.

Trust me, I know a little bit about this one. On the day my wife found out that she was pregnant, she had gotten up early to take her pregnancy test. She was only one day late, but like any woman trying to conceive, she was as neurotic as Woody Allen. She crawled out of bed, peed on the stick, and got back into bed clutching it as carefully as if it were a bottle of nitroglycerin. After three minutes, she saw the two lines that she had been praying for and knew that she was pregnant. She woke me expecting a tearful Kodak moment, but instead got my groggy response of, "I'm glad, Hon." Then I kissed her in the general proximity of her face, rolled over, and went back to sleep.

You may think I'm a loser, but the truth is, she had had a miscarriage a few months before, and I didn't want to get my hopes up again. But the damage was done and she'll never let me forget it. So learn from my mistake and give her that Kodak moment. Women seem to live for those things. That and gossip magazines that expose celebrities with cellulite.

Once you get past that hurdle, the realization will set in. You did it. You finally got your wife pregnant! You can now lift your head higher, broaden your chest, and ruffle your feathers in pride. You now realize that you are indeed capable of creating a new life (with a little help from your wife and God). My heartiest congratulations!

I

The First Month

Now that the arduous task of conception is over, you're about to step into even rougher waters—a tsunami, really, called pregnancy. If you think your part in the reproductive process is over, you're sorely mistaken. Although it's true that carrying the child is indeed women's work, you, my friend, will be carrying a big share of the burden.

This fact may come as a surprise. From what you've seen in movies and episodes of *Mad Men,* you may think pregnancy is a time for your wife to simply sit back and glow. You'll both fall asleep with your hands on her belly and smiles on your faces. Angels will circle above and there'll be soothing music playing in the background wherever you go. But this little delusion couldn't be further from the truth.

Sure, some men may indeed have a wonderful time over these next nine months. Their wives will love every moment of being pregnant and will suffer very few side effects. But for everyone else, the road of pregnancy is a rough road indeed, filled with exhaustion, crankiness, and many aches and pains. And I don't mean for your wife.

Pregnancy is a time of change—physical, emotional, and, of course, financial. But I am here for you, brother. I've broken down the changes that you may encounter and will go into them at length in the chapters that follow. Not only will you get practical solutions and advice, you'll also get that comforting feeling of knowing that you're not alone. Don't worry: Every man who has sown his seed has gone through the same challenges that you'll face. So get ready: The game of pregnancy is about to begin.

What Goodies Await You This Month

Every month, your wife may experience some of the numerous side effects that pregnancy can bring. If you think that her body's only reaction to getting knocked up will be a bloated belly, think again. It may take a village to raise a kid, but it takes the efforts of your wife's entire body to grow one. Because of this, I'll start off each chapter by including a list of possible side effects that each month may bring and offer suggestions on how you can make your wife feel better. Trust me, fellas, when she feels better, you'll feel better, too.

The Easiest Month

During the first month of pregnancy, husbands get off pretty easy. Your wife may not even know that she's pregnant. That's because pregnancy begins two weeks before the sperm actually makes contact with the egg. Yes, I know that this sounds crazy. It goes against everything you learned in junior-high health class to think that conception began before you had the sex that caused it. But it's true, at least from a medical standpoint.

How can this be? It's because the standard practice for counting the term of a pregnancy is to start with the first day of the woman's last period, which—if your wife has all the charts and graphs for her baby-making project that mine did—will be a specifically known date. By the time you get to the day of your essential role in this procedure, about two weeks will have passed. And it will probably be about another two weeks before your wife wakes you up with her cries of delight after peeing on a stick.

The good news about this confusion is that it makes for one less month of side effects to deal with; it makes the pregnancy last one-ninth less than you expected. And best of all, it allows you to sit on your butt for one extra month!

But don't get too comfortable in your La-Z-Boy recliner just yet. You will have plenty of work ahead of you dealing with your wife's multitude of ailments.

Her Symptoms and What You Can Do about Them

These are some of the side effects that may come about during your wife's first month of pregnancy.

Sore Boobs
- Suggest that your wife replace her underwire bras.
- Keep your hands to yourself! There will be no fondling of any kind.

Fatigue
- Make sure your wife isn't awakened at night.
- Take the phone off the hook, turn the TV off, and take every barking dog in the neighborhood out to the city limits.
- Don't wake her under any circumstance, or you'll experience the wrath of . . .

Mood Swings

Even at this early stage your wife is capable of having mood swings. You may think that they're the usual PMS before her period, but now it's PMS to the nth degree. You should definitely:

- Be understanding. Don't pick fights. If a fight starts, for heaven's sake, let her win! Give her a hug for no reason and throw in an "I love you" for extra credit.
- Offer her a snack to steady her blood sugar level— that way she's less likely to level you.
- Fix her a cup of chamomile tea. Chamomile is a natural relaxant that might take the edge off. In fact, I'd use it at every meal. Sprinkle it over her morning cereal, and use it as an ice cream topping. But because there are conflicting reports of the safety of chamomile during pregnancy (mainly the use of chamomile used as an herbal *drug* during pregnancy), consult your health care provider if your wife is having more than a cup or two a day.

Toodle-oo, Ta-Tas

Sore boobs are the first sign that your wife may be pregnant. It's also the first sign that she may just be having her period. It's a cruel trick Mother Nature likes to play on her innocent daughters desperate to conceive. And Mother Nature has a mean trick up her sleeve for her sons as well.

During the first trimester, your wife's boobs will inflate. If they were the size of a Dixie cup before, they'll balloon to the size of a beer stein now. And they'll grow very tender. Just when they become the most enticing, they also become the most sensitive. They'll hurt when your wife puts on a bra, lies on her stomach, or even stands in front of a fan. Don't even look at them, because you're not going to be able to play with your favorite toys for several months. Sure, all the other men will be jealous when you walk into a room with your voluptuous wife, but little do they know that you'd stand a better chance of getting your hands on the Hope Diamond.

Come next trimester, things might change. By then your wife's breasts won't be so sore—and better still, they'll become even more inflated. But you may feel a bit deflated when she pushes you off her time and time again. That's because some pregnant women not only lose their waistlines, they lose their sex drive as well. But we'll get to that aspect of pregnancy a little bit later in the book.

By the last trimester, you may not even want to get your hands on your wife's breasts. You'll find that if you give them a squeeze, they may leak a few drops of colostrum (practice milk). It's thick and yellow and has the consistency of wood glue. Seeing it may make you lose all desire for sex. But it may inspire you to build that coffee table that you've been putting off for so long.

I know that you don't like having to put your favorite playthings in storage. The only comfort that I can give you is that since some men gain some weight when their wives are pregnant, you may develop a nice pair of knockers to fondle all your own.

What to Expect at the OB's Office

There are two things that you should know right off the bat: OB stands for obstetrician, and yes, you do need to go with your wife to her appointments. You don't have to show up for every visit if you have work obligations, but attend as many as possible. If your time is limited, make sure that you go to the third month's appointment to hear the baby's heartbeat, and be sure to go to any appointment that involves an ultrasound. Seeing your baby on TV makes for a lifelong memory. Keep in mind that unlike other TV personalities, yours won't have the benefit of heavy makeup and backlighting, and its appearance may just scare you silly.

There are several things to prepare yourself for at the doctor's office. First of all, you may feel uncomfortable. The waiting room will be filled with other pregnant women and a few young children of preschool age. The women in the room will stare at you and make you feel uneasy. But allow me to let you in on a little secret. The reason these women are staring is that they're thinking what a wonderful husband you are to come with your wife, and why the hell didn't their guy come along with them? So even though you're feeling a bit out of place, rest assured that somewhere out there is a man who'll be sleeping on the couch tonight, and it won't be you.

Also be prepared for the wall full of pictures of naked women. Unlike the photos *Playboy* runs, these will excite you about as much as seeing your mother naked. These larger-than-life images of the female anatomy break down the reproductive system in minute detail. You'll see the fallopian tubes, ovaries, labia, vulva, and other parts that you never even knew existed. You'll stare at them blankly, much as your wife does when looking at the inside of a car engine. Like you, she never much cared about the individual parts just as long as she could get the engine turned on.

You also should prepare yourself for feeling ignored. Even though the waiting room is filled with magazines, not one of them will interest you. And unlike the visiting toddlers, you will have no toys to play with. Once you make it to the examining room, don't expect things to change. The doctor will pay as much attention to you as he (or she) does to a lab coat. After all, your wife is the patient. She's the one who needs the doctor's advice, comfort, and support. All I can say is get used to this type of neglect. You'll be taking a back seat throughout most of the pregnancy. But don't worry. Things will even out in the end. After the baby is born, it'll be the one who gets all the attention, and your wife will be sitting in the back right along with you.

The last thing to prepare yourself for is the jealousy you'll feel toward the doctor. If her doctor is a man, you may find it upsetting that he's going to see your wife naked (if it's a woman, you may find it somewhat arousing, but that's a matter for a different book). From an anthropological viewpoint, your wife is your "woman" and it's hands-off for the rest of the Neanderthals. But you have to get over it. During some of the tests and throughout the entire delivery process, there'll be a bevy of men getting an up-close and personal look at your spouse. And after the birth, your wife will be flinging out her breasts in order to nurse at every mall, restaurant, and dinner party in the city.

You may feel jealous about the bond that your wife shares with her doctor. You may notice that she gets more excited about going to her OB appointment than to a romantic dinner with you. This will be harder to take if you don't like her doctor much or if he's especially good-looking. But just know that your wife's bond with her doctor is an important one. She has to trust him and know that they're on the same team. And you, my friend, are just the water boy on the playing field of reproduction.

Sex in the First Trimester

If you were part of one of those couples who needed help to conceive, you're already used to having a different kind of sex life. Back then it was days of abstinence, followed by intercourse on her highly fertile days. But if you think that just because your boys were finally able to get the job done your old sex life will return to normal, think again. In fact, things won't be normal in the sack until after the baby's born (I won't make you weep by telling you just how long after). But don't despair: at times, sex may get even better than it was before.

Pregnancy sex usually falls into three distinct phases, with each one following the three distinct trimesters. Because of this, at the beginning of each trimester—in Chapters 1, 4, and 7—I'll explain what surprises may be in store for you.

During this first trimester, you'll no doubt be reminded of your acne-ridden, teenage-angst days of celibacy, because you'll be getting about the same amount of action. This is especially true if your wife is having a lot of morning sickness. Unlike a man, who can get turned on moments after suffering a tractor accident, women find it difficult to get aroused after a day of barfing. In addition, she may have mood swings that result in her getting mad at you quite often. Therefore, if you're hoping to get lucky tonight, you'd better think twice before putting that empty milk container back in the refrigerator instead of in the trash.

The best way to deal with your wife's lack of desire is to appear understanding. Comfort her. Listen to her complaints. And for God's sake, take out the trash. I've learned that doing a little housework will get your wife much more aroused than nibbling on her neck. (Women refer to it as "choreplay.") If men only knew what it is women really wanted, there would be a lot more happy men . . . and sparkling kitchen floors.

Another reason you may be sidelined? Some doctors recommend complete pelvic rest during the first trimester if a miscarriage has previously occurred. And, unfortunately, when her pelvis rests, so does yours.

If you're lucky enough to have a wife who isn't experiencing morning sickness, mood swings, or miscarriages, there are still some other things you should know.

1. **Don't be too concerned if your wife spots** (leaks a few drops of blood through her vagina) during the act of sex. It's fairly common for spotting to occur, especially during the last trimester when the cervix (which is at the bottom of her uterus) is ripening for delivery. The

spotting shouldn't last long, but be sure to call the doctor if it continues for more than a few hours, is accompanied by cramping, or if the bleeding becomes steady.

2. **Sex will *not* cause any harm to your baby.** Not only is
the baby protected by a cushion of amniotic fluid, but
your wife's cervix is also closed up tighter than your
sphincter right before a prostate exam. Besides, not
to shatter your delusions of grandeur, but your penis
just isn't that big.

3. **On the positive side, your wife's low libido during the
first trimester may be the calm before the spectacular
sexual storm.** Come next trimester, her drive could be
so overpowering that you'll be begging her to let you
out of bed occasionally. So take a deep breath and a
cold shower, and wait for the spectacular storm clouds
to arrive.

My Wife as a Dog

A funny thing happened when my wife became pregnant.
She turned into a dog. That's not to say that she became
unattractive. But I did come to the realization that my wife
now had more in common with man's best friend. Pregnancy gave her the nose of a bloodhound and the drooling
capacity of a Saint Bernard (not to mention the vicious snap
of a pit bull).

Although being able to smell the peanuts in a plane fly-
ing overhead might seem like a mighty keen trick, it can be a
cruel joke to a pregnant woman. To begin with, her enhanced
sense of smell makes having to deal with morning sickness
much more difficult. Here your poor wife gets nauseated

just looking at a glass of water, and she's forced to smell Mrs. Rosenthal's boiled cabbage from down the street.

My wife was like a nasal superhero. Sure, Superman could fly, but his powers paled in comparison. I would come home from work and my wife could smell the drop of coffee that I spilled on my pants that morning. She would enter the living room and detect a raisin that had dropped under the sofa during the Clinton administration. The refrigerator was always a source of frustration for her. She would smell that something had gone bad but didn't have the stomach to search for it. So I went in, threw out some sacrificial item, stuck in a new box of baking soda, and hoped for the best. My wife was an irritating yet constant source of amazement.

In addition to her newfound strong olfactory sense, your wife may be drooling more than you do when you pass by a Harley-Davidson showroom. Just hand her the box of tissues without comment.

We can only hope that within a few more generations this evolutionary condition will have run its course and will disappear along with other useless things like our appendix and pinkie toe. That way our pregnant wives won't be so uncomfortable and our carpets won't be so soggy.

How to Live with a Woman with Mood Swings

Mood swings are pretty much a requirement for a pregnant woman. In fact, if your wife doesn't fill her daily quota of them, her pregnancy membership card can be revoked and she'll be denied her union benefits, like having someone give up a seat for her on a crowded bus.

It's pretty much guaranteed that throughout any given day, your wife will feel angry, sad, happy, irate, scared, depressed, and cranky. And her feelings will be magnified like never before, because when a woman is pregnant, her emotions are supersized. Experiencing these daily mood swings is exhausting to live with and can really make pregnancy a miserable experience. Sure the big boob thing is nice, but it doesn't even come close to making up for this horrific side effect of pregnancy.

Luckily for me, my wife was too exhausted by her constant morning sickness to pull off a good mood swing, so I got off pretty easy for the first few months. But man, after that, I was in deep doo-doo. In fact, her mood swing pendulum swung so hard that it got stuck, and remained permanently locked in the "bitch" position for the remainder of her pregnancy. What made matters worse was that just about anything could set her off. One day I'd come home and ask how she was feeling, and she'd yell at me because she was so sick of being asked that question. So the next day I purposely didn't ask her, and she yelled at me even louder because she thought I didn't care. I was always walking a fine line between being inattentive or too attentive, and that line was more dangerous than the San Andreas Fault.

Expressing a mood isn't the only thing that your pregnant wife can do. She also has the uncanny ability to express several of them together. She can feel depressed when she laughs. She can cry when she's mad. She can give you a hug and smack you across the face in the same beat. It really is a freakish thing to behold. The only thing that you can do is accept the fact that until the baby is born, your wife will be temporarily insane and you will be the punching bag at the insane asylum.

I found that the most frustrating thing about mood swings is that women don't even realize that they're having them. All they know is that they're really upset and that it's all your fault. But because of my vast experience, I do have some well-earned pieces of wisdom to share with you:

1. **First and foremost, don't take her mood swings personally.** I know that this is easy to say and hard to do, but if you can distance yourself from your wife's moods emotionally, it will help. If that doesn't work, try distancing yourself from her physically. She may just need a little extra space, and not just because she's the size of a beached whale.

2. **Make sure that you call your wife if you're going to come home late.** One of the emotions that tends to escalate in pregnant women is jealousy. That, combined with the superhuman sense of smell, can make for a suspicious creature. If you've so much as hugged another woman or simply walked past a perfume counter, she's sure to pick up the scent and grill you like never before.

3. **No matter what you do, don't tell a pregnant woman that she's just mad because she's having a mood swing.** It's sure to set her off even more. It's just like back in the old days when your wife had PMS and became cranky. But if you told her that she was upset because she had PMS, she'd explode. It was like pouring gasoline on a fire. And right now your wife is like one big bloated bonfire waiting for you to douse her with fuel.

4. **Drink heavily.** But do it in private so it won't piss her off.

Your Pregnancy Survival Kit

Follow the Boy Scout motto: Be Prepared. When you're faced with a desperate situation, you must pack those items essential to your survival. You already know that you need mosquito repellent when traipsing in an African jungle, shark repellent while on a leaky raft, and insurance-seller repellent for your high school reunion. Pregnancy is no less of a desperate situation, and you must enter into it prepared. Your pregnancy survival kit should contain the basic items that you'll need in order to live through this dangerous and often life-threatening situation.

Anyone who's read *National Geographic* knows that wild animals attack for two main reasons (they also know that tribal women like to walk around topless, but that's just an added bonus):

Reason #1: The animal is in pain.

Reason #2: The animal is hungry.

Your pregnant woman is in a constant state of pain and hunger. Because of this, she should be treated like any other savage creature ready to attack.

Because you never know when an incident will take place, you should keep this survival kit near you at all times. Carry it in your car. Keep it in your closet. Store it under your bed. Your kit should contain the following items to keep your beast feeling her best:

1. **A heating pad** for sciatica and leg cramps.

2. **Saline spray** for her nasal congestion and nosebleeds.

3. **Supplies for giving her a much-appreciated back or foot massage,** such as massage oil and maybe one of those wooden massage thingies for rolling on her back. But be cautious about giving anything more than a simple "at-home" massage. Leave it to the experts to provide therapeutic massage or anything that involves essential oils or non-side-lying positions.

4. **A plastic container filled with nutritious snacks to ward off nausea and any mood swings caused by her low blood sugar.** A mixture of protein and carbs works best, like nuts and crackers or protein bars. Avoid snacks full of sugar, to also avoid the inevitable crash, and lots of salt, to prevent water retention.

5. **A doctor-prescribed antihistamine** for her congestion and to make her drowsy on sleepless nights so that you both can get some rest.

6. **A doctor-prescribed pain medication** like Tylenol for headaches—both hers and yours.

7. **A box of tissues** for the inevitable crying jags and to sop up some of the aforementioned drool.

8. **A doctor-approved stool softener** if she has severe constipation or hemorrhoids.

With this kit in hand, you'll always be prepared to face an attack. For instance, if your wife gets a painful leg cramp, plug in the heating pad, stat! Even if it doesn't do much to relieve her pain, you can still use it as a shield to protect yourself as she hurls nearby items toward your face. With these staples handy, you should always be able to defend yourself against the savage beast that is your wife.

Your "Yes-Yes" List

On your wife's first visit with her OB, she'll be given a list of
things to abstain from throughout her pregnancy (and even
longer if she plans on breastfeeding). Her "no-no" list will
include many of her favorite indulgences such as caffeine,
alcohol, sushi, and, the most painful of all, hair dye.

You, on the other hand, are lucky. You won't be handed
any such list. You can go about your day, the proud dad-to-
be, and never have to deny yourself a thing. Unfortunately,
while you may not have to *give up* anything, you're definitely
going to have to *give*.

Instead of a "no-no" list, you have a "yes-yes" list. On
it are various new tasks that you must perform during the
duration of the pregnancy because your wife cannot.

1. **Change the kitty litter.** Pregnant women are susceptible
   to toxoplasmosis (a parasitic disease that's found in cat
   crap) because of their weakened immune system.
2. **Do any household cleaning that requires using a toxic
   cleaner like oven cleaner, or even strong-smelling ammo-
   nia or chlorine, which may cause nausea.** When using
   these types of cleaners, do so in a well-ventilated room.
   Natural cleaners are great to use when pregnant.
3. **Fill up her car with gasoline when you can.** Although this
   is not an absolute necessity, your wife shouldn't breathe
   in the strong chemical fumes when she can avoid it.
4. **Paint the baby's room.** Painting also involves strong
   chemical fumes.
5. **Do all of the heavy lifting.** It's best if your wife avoids
   lifting anything more than 15 pounds.

6. **Do any chore that requires a ladder.** Pregnant women lose their balance more easily because their center of gravity is constantly shifting.

I know this seems like a lot to do. And yes, most of the items on the yes-yes list will take some time and effort on your part. They may require some thought, maybe even some manual labor, but remember, unlike your wife, you can do most of the things on your list drunk.

Let the Bodily Functions Begin

FADE UP: It's your wedding day. The orchestra is playing. Your beautiful bride is walking toward you in her flowing beaded gown (which could've made for a nice down payment on a house, but you need to let that go). You try to hold back tears as you realize that you're the luckiest man in the world.

DISSOLVE TO PRESENT DAY: This once angelic creature is now big and bloated and filled with more gas than the Hindenburg. She burps and farts wherever she goes. Again, you hold back tears, but these tears are caused by the acrid scent that burns your nasal hairs with every breath. It seems that your bride has now become a walking version of the campfire scene from *Blazing Saddles*.

This sudden transformation from radiant beauty to gassy beast is caused by a miraculous event—this one taking place in your wife's colon. Now that she's pregnant, her entire digestive system has slowed down so it can extract every crucial vitamin and mineral to pass on to your growing baby. Although this digestive change gives your baby the nourishment it needs, it also gives your wife a hell of a lot of gas. And this gas is like none that you've ever known before. It's the rocket fuel of gasses. She could propel herself into orbit with just one big fart.

To make matters worse, your wife no longer thinks that her body is hers anymore. It now belongs to your child, and she is just the landlord. Because of this, she doesn't feel responsible for any of the functions her body performs, and does things now that she would never have dreamed of doing in the past. Before your wife conceived, she may have been too shy to even fart in front of you. Now she farts *on* you.

This internal combustion also enables her to make a belching noise that's almost nonhuman. It's not quite a burp, not quite a hiccup, but a combination of the two. It's loud and irritating and constant. My wife made this noise all the time. She wasn't even aware that she was doing it, but I sure was. I found it to be the most irritating when we were at the movies. Nearby patrons would give us the "Will you please die now?" kind of glare.

Slower digestion also results in constipation. It seems that her bowels are backed up, so her number-one goal is to go number two. She pushes so hard that she fears she's going to projectile-poop out the baby. Because of all that straining, the hemorrhoids are soon to follow. I know you think a problem like hemorrhoids can't possibly be your concern, but you're sadly mistaken. Don't be surprised if she asks you to apply her witch hazel pads or to give her an enema. I can't think of a more dramatic way to erase the romantic image of your bride than to stuff a plastic tube up her butt.

Living with a pregnant woman made me finally understand why couples get emotional when looking back at the photographs of their wedding day. The women tear up because they fear that they'll never fit into their dress again, and the men cry because they remember the glowing woman they once married. Sure, their wives are still glowing, but it's the kind of glow that can only be achieved by trying to hold in a powerful explosive.

They Grow Up So Fast . . . Especially in Utero

What exactly is going on in your wife's soon-to-expand belly? For the next eight chapters, I'll provide you with an inside look at your offspring so you can better understand the unseen, and (frankly) unbelievable, developments.

At some point during the middle of this first month, your child was conceived. Not long after you gave your wife her minimum allowance of post-coital cuddling, your sperm was well on its way for a meet-and-greet with the egg. Several hours after you penetrated your wife, the egg too was penetrated, and the circle of life began spinning its microscopic little wheels. At first your baby was called a "zygote" (a fine name to consider if you're having a boy), but it didn't stay that way for long. About a week later it implanted itself into its new womb, hung up a few posters, and was then called an "embryo."

By the end of this first month, your wife has started to grow a bit tired. Your baby, on the other hand, has started to grow its brain, spinal cord, and head. By the time this first month comes to a close, your little bundle of joy is about the size of a grain of rice—but you and your wife will be feeling its presence in a much bigger way.

2

The Second Month

I'm willing to bet that you didn't buy this book for yourself. Chances are, your wife gave it to you so you'd know what to expect during her pregnancy. You thanked her, but deep down you thought, "Why should I have to read a book about yucky girly things? Besides, how tough can it be to live through a pregnancy?" You figured that trillions of men before you have done it and they survived just fine (of course, most of them are dead now, but this had nothing to do with their wives being pregnant).

Maybe at this early stage you're right. You don't need any help. And you naively think that if things get sticky down the road, your wife will provide you with the comfort and support you'll need to survive. That may be fine in theory, but the truth is that your wife will be of no help to you at all during these next long months. It's not that she doesn't want to be. It's just that she'll be the reason you'll need help.

Not only will your wife be hormonal and riddled with physical ailments, but she may be overwhelmed by dealing with the mental effects of pregnancy. She's worried about what her body will be transformed into. Will it be covered with stretch marks, acne, and varicose veins? Will you still find her attractive after she's been plagued by the battle scars that pregnancy can inflict? She may be concerned that her pain threshold won't be high enough. Can she manage the aches of midnight leg cramps and the constant sciatica? What about the inevitable backaches, hemorrhoids, and headaches? In addition, will she have the willpower to abstain from life's guilty pleasures, like that second cup of coffee or that relaxing glass of Chardonnay at the end of the day?

Pregnancy can be a stressful time for a woman, and therefore for you as well. If it's true that misery loves company, you two should act like newlyweds. But as you can see, your wife may be too busy with her own pains and concerns and too preoccupied by her own crap to care much about yours. That's where I come in. I'll be there to step in on her behalf, to let you know what to expect during these next months. I will listen when you need someone to talk to. Granted, you'll have to speak up really loud so I can hear you where I live, but go ahead and give it a try. With that said, let's plunge ahead into the second month, and see what changes you can expect.

What Goodies Await You This Month

During pregnancy, symptoms can vary more than they can for any other physical condition a person may have. For example, when you get a cold, you can expect to have a sore throat and a runny nose, and to hack up a few loogies from time to time. But with pregnancy, it's a medical free-for-all. Some women will have morning sickness, while others have sciatica. Some will get hemorrhoids, while others develop varicose veins. Some will turn into horndogs, while others will simply crave corndogs. In sum, when a woman is expecting, she can expect many different things.

While some symptoms like morning sickness almost always appear in the first trimester, others, like leg cramps, can strike at any time. Pregnant women are like snowflakes: no two are alike. So even if I mention a certain ailment, it doesn't mean that your wife's going to get it in the same month that I'm talking about—or that she's going to get it at all.

Even if your wife does have some of these difficulties, she doesn't have to have them alone. You can do some things to make your wife feel a little less miserable. Don't expect these helpful hints to work miracles, though. The only miracle you can expect from these nine months of hell will be your baby. But there are some things that you can do to help take the edge off. And even if your attempts to help her fail, at least your wife will see that you're trying, and she may even reward you with some occasional sex, or at least yell at you less often. So punch in that time card, fellas, and let's get to work.

Her Symptoms and What You Can Do about Them

Pregnancy will be easier on both of you if you can find simple ways to help your wife deal with the side effects. Following are some ideas to get you started.

Morning Sickness
- Fix her a plate of protein and carbohydrates, like cheese and crackers. At night, put a plate of crackers on her nightstand and when she wakes up, remind her to eat a few before she gets out of bed.

- Buy her Sea-Bands, which are soft wristbands with acupressure points. You can purchase them at drugstores.
- Offer her a bite of a lemon wedge.
- Brew her a cup of ginger tea, or get her some crystallized ginger from the health-food store. Ginger is a natural nausea reliever.
- Make her any comfort food that she requests (mac-and-cheese and mashed potatoes are always good standbys and—bonus!—they come in a box).
- If her doctor approves, make sure she has medications like Dramamine, Benadryl, Emetrol, and Unisom on hand, along with vitamin B6, to calm her system and reduce her nausea.
- Suggest that she not take her prenatal vitamins all at once. Have her try half in the morning, half at night. Remind her to take them with food.
- If her vitamins still give her problems, ask her doctor if she can just take the folic acid supplement.
- When she's in the car with you, drive more smoothly and steer clear of those stomach-upsetting bumps.
- Stay out of her way when she makes a beeline for the bathroom.

Increased Sense of Smell
- Don't wear cologne. Don't let anyone in the neighborhood wear cologne, either.
- Do the grocery shopping.
- Do all the cooking (and of course the dishes, pots, and pans, but you probably don't need me to tell you that).
- Gas up the car so she won't have to.

- Brush your teeth often. Have everyone in the neighborhood brush their teeth often, too.
- If you smoke, stop. (And of course, make everyone in the neighborhood stop smoking, too!)

Headaches
- Give her Tylenol (if her doctor approves).
- Apply a cold compress to her forehead.
- Rub her temples.
- Push the acupressure point on her hand between that fleshy part of her thumb and forefinger (you can try to convince her that her breasts are acupressure points too, but I don't think she'll fall for it).
- Light a candle with a scent like lavender that's geared for relaxation.
- Have her take a warm bath (make sure the water temperature isn't too hot, since you don't want her uterus turning into a Jacuzzi).
- Encourage her to drink plenty of water.
- Make her a light, healthy snack to elevate her blood sugar level.
- Take a walk with her and hold her hand.
- Make dinner (or at least bring home her favorite take-out) so she can relax.

Gas—And Not the Kind You Find at the Quick-Shop
- Sleep in the other room.
- Toss out any food that contains beans. The effect could burn a hole in her undies.
- Don't light a match in her presence.
- Run for the hills.

Constant Need to Pee
- Find out where the restrooms are ahead of time at every restaurant, movie theater, and event that you go to.
- If you wish to live, don't say, "Not again!"
- Put up nightlights to mark the path to the bathroom.

How to Live with a Woman with Morning Sickness

Morning sickness is one of the most challenging side effects of pregnancy. Not every woman will be affected by this condition. Some may never feel sick. Others may be able to ward off any nausea by eating a cracker. But for other women, morning sickness can strike fast and furious, and it can make the first trimester a horrible one for both of you.

Although experts don't agree on what causes morning sickness, they do agree on one thing: It can make your wife feel very sick. She may vomit at a moment's notice. She may not be able to eat much and may avoid being around food most of the time. And contradictory to its name, morning sickness can make her feel this way any time of the day or night.

You, on the other hand, will be affected by morning sickness in a different way. For you it means waking up to the sound of puking, making your own meals, and eating them alone in the garage so that the smell won't set her off. It also means feeling helpless as you watch your wife "call Huey on the big white phone," or "ride the porcelain Honda," or whatever your favorite euphemism is for what you used to do after those three-keg parties in college.

Because your wife is feeling sick day after day after day, she won't have the strength to care about much of anything. She won't have the energy to get out of bed, and if she ever does, all she'll do is lounge around and watch TV. Your caring, tender, nurturing wife will act just like, well, you. And you, my friend, will have to act like your wife. Until she feels better, you'll have to do all the dishes, pay the bills, and clean the house. You alone will be responsible for taking care of the pets, ironing the clothes, writing all the thank-you notes, and tackling the grease on your kitchen stove.

You can't do anything to make morning sickness go away. Doctors are hesitant to prescribe medications to a pregnant woman for fear that the baby will be born really ugly and they'll get sued. So the average miserable woman has a limited ability to do much of anything. You can try a few things to make her feel better (see the list in the section called "Her Symptoms and What You Can Do about Them" in this chapter). Chances are that none of these things will take away her nausea completely. You'll just have to wait it out. In most cases, morning sickness ends around the start of the second trimester.

Some cases of morning sickness are quite severe and may last through the entire pregnancy. The technical term for this condition is "hyperemesis." Women with hyperemesis have a problem keeping any food down and tend to lose a lot of weight. They can become dehydrated and may even need hospitalization. In these severe cases, doctors may prescribe anti-nausea medications.

The old wives have spun many tales about morning sickness. They say it's a good way to determine the sex of your baby before it's born. If your wife has a pretty rough bout of morning sickness, then she's going to give birth to a girl; if not, then a boy. I know the old broads were right in our case. My wife was so nauseated for the first three months that I thought she'd pop out enough girls to make a softball team.

I know the period of morning sickness seems endless, but trust me, there will come a day when your wife will look a little less green. One day, usually around the fourteenth week of pregnancy, she will lift her head up out of the toilet bowl and have the strength to nag at you once again. In the meantime, give her whatever she needs and realize that although you have a lot more chores to do, you're actually pretty lucky. It's hard for your wife to have a wide range of moods when she can barely lift her head off the pillow.

Crib Notes

Don't worry. This segment isn't about how to buy the right crib, although while we're on the subject, for safety reasons, you should never use a crib with bars set far enough apart that you can pass a beer can through the slats. The space between the bars should be no wider than 2½ inches. Not that you'd pass your baby a beer can anyway. But I digress.

The gestation period is not unlike a school term. You have a lot of facts to memorize, and many tests to take. And believe me, you don't want to fail one of these tests.

Pregnancy is full of medical mumbo-jumbo and technical terms that you've never used in daily conversation, unless you're a med student or have a warped sense of humor ("a labia and vulva went into a bar . . ."). Your wife, on the other hand, has become quite the learned student—so much so that she'll become *your* teacher. Although she may be cute in a dominatrix kind of way, you'll find her more intimidating than any teacher you've ever had. She's read all the books and talked with the doctors. She's as fluent in the language of pregnancy as she is in Italian (shoe designers, that is).

The main reason that your wife is so strict on the subject of pregnancy is that she has a warped belief system. She assumes that how much baby jargon you know is in direct proportion with how much you care about your baby. The way she sees it is that if you're not familiar with a certain pregnancy term, then you're not taking the proper interest in your child. If she's talking about sciatica and you think she's referring to a prison in upstate New York, you will be expelled from the class and from the bedroom.

But luckily, just like back in your old school days, you can cheat. I'm going to pass along the crib notes that I collected during my wife's pregnancy, covering the various pregnancy terms, tests, and conditions that you'll need to know to ace this nine-month course. I suggest that you keep this list in your library (otherwise known as the top of your toilet tank) for quick reference. This way, if your wife pulls a "sciatica" on you, just tell her you have to pee, run to the bathroom, and refer to these definitions. You'll come out of there rattling off this odd language like a linguistics major.

These crib notes don't encompass every pregnancy term that there is, just the most common ones. If your wife expects you to know terms like *caput succedaneum*, then I think she's expecting too much from you, and you can tell her I said so.

Pregnancy Tests
- **Amniocentesis:** A test to detect genetic malformations. A small amount of amniotic fluid is removed and studied to determine chromosomal mutations and the baby's gender.

- **CVS:** This stands for "chorionic villus sampling," not the popular drugstore chain. It's a test to detect genetic disorders. It's used instead of an amniocentesis and can be performed earlier than the amnio as well. This test is also much less invasive.
- **Glucose screen:** A one-hour test done about the twenty-sixth week of pregnancy to detect possible gestational diabetes.
- **Glucose tolerance:** A three-hour test done to detect possible gestational diabetes that is performed only if your wife fails the glucose screen.

Pregnancy Conditions
- **Carpal tunnel syndrome:** A painful and numbing condition caused by the swelling of an inflamed ligament in the wrist.
- **Edema:** A condition that makes your wife swell up to the size of the Stay-Puft Marshmallow Man from *Ghostbusters*.
- **Hyperemesis:** A case of severe morning sickness that may or may not continue throughout the duration of the pregnancy.
- **Incompetent cervix:** A condition wherein the cervix unexpectedly opens up and causes a miscarriage.
- **Incontinence:** The ailment that your wife shares with your grandma: the ability to pee in their pants when they cough, sneeze, laugh, or make any sudden bodily movements.
- **Leukorrhea:** The thick vaginal discharge that she'll have throughout pregnancy. Big yuck, I know.

- **Placenta previa:** A condition in which the placenta is attached to the upper or lower portion of the uterus and not in the center, where all good placentas should be.
- **Sciatica:** A pain in her tush caused by pressure on the sciatic nerve, which runs through her butt and down her leg.
- **Toxemia:** Elevated blood pressure. This is also known as pre-eclampsia or eclampsia and can be particularly dangerous for the baby.
- **Varicose veins:** This unpleasant condition is caused by a pool of blood trapped in a vein located somewhere from her leg up to her vulva.

Pregnancy Terms

- **Amniotic fluid:** The fluid that the baby floats in while inside the womb.
- **Apgar score:** Immediately after the baby is born, he or she is tested for basic skills like reflex and the ability to pee on you during a diaper change.
- **Birth canal:** It's basically just another term for vagina, but it's easier to say when your father-in-law is in the room.
- **Braxton-Hicks:** Practice contractions that your wife will start having around the seventh month.
- **Breech:** A baby that's in the "heads up" position.
- **Cesarean section:** Surgically removing the baby through an incision in your wife's belly instead of having the baby come out of her vagina.
- **Colostrum:** The forerunner of breast milk.
- **Couvade syndrome:** Sympathy pains you may experience that are similar to your wife's pregnancy ailments.

- **Epidural anesthesia:** A girl's best friend. It's a pain-killer administered directly in her back to take the "labor" out of labor.
- **Episiotomy:** A cut in your wife's vagina to allow more room for your baby's big old head to pass through her little old vagina.
- **False labor:** When your wife's uterus starts to contract for a length of time but then stops suddenly because your baby gets stage fright.
- **Kegels:** Pelvic exercises your wife can perform to help strengthen her muscles for delivery. They can also make sex more fun, not that you'll ever get to find out.
- **Lamaze class:** A waste of time and money.
- **Maternity clothes:** One of the big frustrations of pregnancy. They cost a fortune and will only be worn for the length of a football season.
- **Quickening:** Feeling the baby move in her womb.

This cheat sheet is sure to teach you the basic things necessary to pass your class. If you study hard, you may even become the teacher's pet and get to do some petting of your own. At the very least, I hope you learn something that, unlike in all the other classes you took, you may actually use in real life.

Now You're Cookin'!

There are plenty of things that I'm good at around the house. I can unclog a drain. I can change a light fixture. I can even fix the garbage disposal if all it needs is to have the reset button pushed. But one thing I can't do is cook. My wife is, and always has been, the cook in the family. She makes all my favorites, from smothered pork chops to pigs-in-a-blanket. But once the morning sickness set in, the only thing that was wrapped in a blanket was my wife.

So it was either sauté or get off the pot. I realized that I had to learn some culinary basics or starve trying. I glanced through my wife's cookbooks and found a brownie recipe that seemed fairly simple, but I still messed up. It seems I don't know my ass from my aspic and I couldn't understand the instructions. Why do they say "mix by hand" if they really don't want you to use your hand? They could just as easily say "mix by fork" if that's what they want you to do. So I had to rethink my plan.

I discovered a wonderful solution: precooked foods. Instead of actually cooking, I just combined stuff that's already cooked. I took advantage of living in an era in which precooked foods are readily available in most markets and ran with it. I went to the store and loaded up on supplies. I started with a few basic staples and mixed them in various ways to create a wide range of delicious dishes. If you can boil water, you, too, can make casseroles, entrées, pasta dishes, and stir-fries. Even though life was giving me lemons I could now make lemonade, lemon bars, lemon chutney, and lemon chicken.

The basic theory of my culinary wisdom is to combine four ingredients: a protein, a vegetable, a starch, and a sauce. Get organic ingredients whenever possible, as well as those low in sodium, fat, and sugar. The one hard and fast rule is to make sure that everything you buy is precooked. You can buy nonfat versions if you wish, but personally, I don't like them. I think nonfat foods should include a nonflavor warning.

Here are some of the basic ingredients.

Protein

Eating protein is a must for a pregnant woman. In fact, it can be the strongest of all food cravings. I've seen many a vegetarian cross over to the dark (aka meat-eating) side when they become pregnant. Here are some suggestions from this necessary and tempting food group:

- **Whole cooked chicken**—supermarkets usually have a heater full of whole roasted or BBQ birds
- **Packaged grilled chicken breast slices** sold in the deli section
- **Precooked sausage** in the meat department
- **Canned tuna**
- **Canned salmon** (no more than once a week)
- **Canned chicken** (It may sound funky but it really is pretty good. Back in our single days, we all ate worse things.)
- **Frozen meatballs**
- **Soy dogs** (Because of new concerns, use moderation when using soy products since it may mess with estrogen levels. Consult your OB if your wife plans on eating a lot of soy products.)
- **Soy meatballs**
- **Frozen shrimp**
- **Frozen scallops**
- **Prepackaged grated cheese**

Vegetables

Most all fresh veggies are easy to cut up into small pieces to cook, but if even that frightens you they have prepackaged, precut frozen vegetables that only need to be tossed in the microwave or thrown into the pot of boiling pasta water for the last few minutes. Canned veggies should be your last resort since they usually are the least nutritious. When using fresh, be sure to wash them thoroughly—listeria, a bacteria found in foods like uncooked vegetables, can cause complications for pregnant women. These are a few of your choices:

- **Bagged shredded carrots and/or cabbage** in the salad section of the produce department
- **Bagged spinach leaves and salad lettuces** in the salad section
- **Presliced mushrooms**
- **Frozen peas, corn, and other veggies**
- **Olives**

Starch

What's more enjoyable than eating a big bowl of starch? Eating carbs may sound horrifying to many Atkins diet followers, but it seems to be the most comforting to a pregnant woman. Give these a try:

- **Any shape or size dried pasta or noodle**—just boil water
- **Fresh or frozen ravioli** and other pastas
- **Instant rice** (You don't have to use instant, but why make life any tougher than it is right now? They may even sell precooked rice in your market's freezer section—all you need to do is nuke.)
- **Crescent roll dough or premade pizza dough**
- **Refrigerated or frozen pie crust**

Sauce

No, the FDA doesn't stipulate a recommended daily allowance for sauce, but since it tastes so darn good, why not throw in a ladle full of it for good measure? If weight gain is an issue, stay away from cream sauce or use a low-fat version. If heartburn's a problem, avoid tomato sauce. These are a few possibilities:

- **Canned or jarred tomato sauce**
- **Cream soups** like chicken, mushroom, broccoli, or asparagus
- **Premade pesto sauce or alfredo sauce** sold with the fresh pastas
- **Bottled teriyaki and other Asian-food sauces**

Now the combining technique comes into play. Take one or more items from each column and combine it with the others. Here are some examples.

Calzone

Open a roll of premade crescent roll dough. Flatten it out onto a cookie sheet and pour on enough tomato sauce to cover the top of the dough. Add precooked sausage, sliced mushrooms, and a handful of shredded cheese. Fold the dough in half and press the edges together to seal. Put it in a 350°F oven until the crust is brown and your kitchen smells like your local Pizza Hut.

Tuna Noodle Casserole

In a large casserole dish, mix a can of tuna with a dollop of mayonnaise, a can of creamed condensed soup (mushroom, asparagus, or broccoli all work well), a handful of your favorite shredded cheese, and a splash of Worcester-shire sauce. Toss in a handful of frozen peas, pour in some cooked noodles, and mix it all together. Add another handful of cheese on top and pop into a 350°F oven until bubbly and delicious. (For a variation, you can substitute canned chicken for the tuna.)

Quiche

Bake a frozen pie shell according to the package directions. While it's baking, mix three eggs with a cup and a half of cream (or milk). Add a handful of cheese, some cut-up precooked veggies like mushrooms, spinach, broccoli, or asparagus (anything but tomatoes), salt, pepper, and, if you want to be extra fancy, a dash of nutmeg. Put in a 350°F oven until lightly browned on top.

Pasta Dishes

Pasta dishes are the most versatile. All you have to do is boil a large pot of water and add your pasta. While it's cooking, open a can of tomato sauce or alfredo sauce and put it in a saucepan. Put the heat on low and add cooked and diced chicken, sausage, or meatballs, plus a handful of green olives, spinach, or mushroom slices (or whatever veggies you like) to the sauce. Drain the cooked pasta and put it back in the pot. Add the sauce and combine. Top with shredded cheese, and *bon appétit*.

You could also drizzle some oil in a skillet and add some cooked instant rice or leftover rice from last night's Chinese dinner. Toss in some frozen peas and a handful of shredded carrots and cabbage. Add about half a cup of water or broth and cook on low heat for about five minutes. Once warmed, add some cooked chicken, pour on some teriyaki sauce, and you'll have a delicious stir-fry meal. The possibilities for cooking by combining these elements are endless.

Natural Remedies

If you want to help your wife with some of her pregnancy ailments, include some of the following foods in your recipes—or even on the side.

For Morning Sickness
- **Ginger:** It's a natural nausea reliever. You can buy pickled ginger at your grocer's sushi counter, or crystallized ginger from your local health-food store. You can also buy it fresh from the produce section and use it sparingly to spice up your recipes. There is also ginger tea or natural ginger ale.
- **Raspberries:** They too are said to help with morning sickness. Serve them fresh or make them into milkshakes. Some women with morning sickness do well with milkshakes.
- **Lemon and basil:** These seasonings can also ease nausea.
- **Peppermint:** Have a bunch of peppermint drops handy and offer them at the end of each meal.

For Constipation
- **Fiber:** If your wife is constipated, think fiber. Most veggies and fruits are good sources of fiber, as is whole grain bread and, of course, prune juice. Avoid processed foods, since they usually contain the least amount of fiber.
- **Water:** Make sure to serve a big glass of H_2O with every meal. Staying hydrated helps keep her system running smoothly.

- **Avoid certain foods:** Dairy, fast food, and fried foods are all known to cause constipation.

For Leg Cramps
- **Bananas, avocados, chard, and lentils** are good sources of potassium, which pregnant women are often lacking.
- **Cheese, milk, and broccoli** are good sources of calcium, which pregnant women are often lacking.

Even after my wife's morning sickness passed, she still wasn't up to cooking much, so I wore the chef's hat for the duration of her pregnancy. Once our baby was born, the hat was retired and put on permanent loan to our favorite Chinese takeout restaurant.

How to Be a Domestic God

Before your wife got pregnant, you may have lucked out when it came to doing your share of household chores. I know I did. Sure, I had to unload the dishwasher from time to time or do a load of laundry when I ran out of clean socks. But because of my good negotiating skills (aka "sheer begging"), my wife did most of the housework. It all seemed to work out well until that egg told my sperm to come on in and stay awhile, and ruined a perfectly good system. You too may notice that now that your wife is with child, you are with dishpan hands.

I'm sure that you understand how difficult it is for a pregnant woman to run a house. She's nauseated and has a hard time cooking and doing the shopping. She's tired and doesn't have the energy to dust the furniture. She's forbidden to use household cleaners that contain strong solvents, and soon, she'll get so big that she won't even be able to see the floor to vacuum it.

When your wife first starts asking you to help out around the house, you may readily agree, assuming that if a man can build a house, it shouldn't be such a big deal to run it. Soon you'll realize the truth. Running it is much harder. Not only are there the basic household demands like cooking, cleaning, and laundry, but there are also required field trips to the drugstore, the post office, the dry cleaners, and the vet's. There are checkbooks to balance, plants to water, and repairs to schedule. The to-do list is endless.

I know it seems a bit overwhelming, so let me turn this mountain into a dust bunny so that you can sweep it under the rug and forget about it. Once again, I want to pass along some words of wisdom to help you make your new road just a little more sanitary and pine-smelling. Take off that tool belt and strap on an apron, men. We've got some housework to do.

Going to the Grocery Store

Before you hit the grocery aisles, you must make a list of the things you need to buy. Seems simple, right? Not so fast, my friend. Once you're at the market, you'll be amazed at all of the selection you'll be faced with for the same type of item. Take bologna, for instance. Did you know that there's beef bologna, chicken bologna, pork bologna, low-fat bologna, and fat-free bologna—and they all come in both thick-sliced and thin-sliced versions? The variety approaches infinity. That's why your list must be as detailed as possible. It's not going too far to photograph the items you need to replace and take those pictures with you to the store. (Finally! A use for your cell phone camera now that your wife won't let you take those naked pictures anymore!)

Doing the Laundry

It sounds so simple. Whites go in hot water. Colors go in cold. But then there were a lot of in-between colors like grays and khakis that I was never quite sure what to do with. I threw all of those unsure things in warm and prayed to the laundry gods that it would work out okay.

Instead of praying, you may find it helpful to use those laundry sheets that absorb color dye. Nothing will piss your wife off more than if her whites are tinted red because you washed them with your Chiefs football shirt.

My biggest tip of all: if you wash something that's lacy, or turns you on in any way, *do not* put it in the dryer. Drape it from the shower rod. For bonus points, put a towel underneath it to absorb the water.

Cleaning the Kitchen

You've already realized that you're going to have to start doing the cooking. If you've had little experience in the food-prep milieu in the past, don't start getting too fancy now. Think simple. One-pot meals are easy and require the least amount of cleanup. Get a cookbook of thirty-minute meals or slow-cooker meals, or better yet, try some of my recipes from the previous section.

Warning: Don't put onion skins, celery stalks, or anything stringy down the garbage disposal. This will mess it up way past the reset button trick. With what you pay the plumber you could have dined out for a week at four-star restaurants.

Shopping at the Drugstore

A pregnant woman needs many supplies from the drugstore. And they're not going to be macho supplies like arm slings and jock-itch cream. Nope. They're going to be hardcore embarrassing crap like hemorrhoid cream, stool softeners, and panty shields, all of which will test the limits of your masculinity. My advice is to make sure that the prices of these items are clearly marked. The last thing you need is for the cashier to run a price check for incontinence pads through the PA system.

I do have a shopping suggestion that will make your life easier, but it goes against every male instinct that you have—you know, things like never asking for directions while driving or help when you're manning the grill. I suggest that you ask someone who works at either the supermarket or the drugstore to help you. I know you don't want to, but it really does work. Invariably you'll find someone sporting a nametag and bow tie who can unlock the secrets to the hidden whereabouts of your to-do list. He is the gatekeeper of household errands. Maybe you think he'll laugh at you. Maybe you're afraid he'll think you're less of a warrior if you don't know the secret location of the nipple cream. But step up to the plate and give it a try. Your life will be much easier.

After a time, you'll become quite adept at taking care of the house. You'll run it with the precision of a quarterback throwing a bomb into the end zone. But you can never let your wife in on that fact. You should never appear too competent. Never get the whites too white, or the shirts too wrinkle-free. If your wife is aware of how good you've actually become at taking care of the house, the job will be yours forever.

The "I'm So Hungry I Could Eat Your Face" Syndrome

When the proprietors of an all-you-can-eat restaurant see a pregnant woman heading toward their doors, they want to hang out the "closed" sign and turn out all the lights. They know that once this woman hits the buffet, they're going to lose money, and lose it big.

By now, you know a thing or two about dealing with the eating habits of a pregnant woman. You don't stand in front of the refrigerator. You don't mention that she just ate ten minutes ago. And you don't say, "My God, you're like a toad. You're eating three times your weight in food every day."

Why is your wife acting like she just finished a hunger strike? First, her body needs more calories than it did before. Even when your wife is sitting still, she's burning more calories than a rock climber. On average, a pregnant woman needs to eat about 300 extra calories a day, and she'll take full advantage of every single one. Can you blame her, really? For a woman's entire life she's been taught by society that she needs to be slender. Some women walk away from every meal feeling hungry and unsatisfied in a desperate attempt to resemble the models on magazine covers. Now, after all these years of denying herself, a woman is finally set free. At long last, she can give in to temptation, and even has doctor's orders to eat for two! She feels as happy as you'd be if your doctor told you that you are medically required to drink beer for two.

Second, when the urge to eat hits her, it hits her hard. Her blood sugar can drop faster than Michael Vick's fan base during the dog-fighting scandal. So when she needs to eat, she needs to eat *now*.

In this state, she becomes a threat to herself and mankind. She ravages through the cupboards throwing empty containers in her wake. She's become Charlie Sheen, and the pantry has become every stripper in Vegas.

Although your wife's eating habits may be a bit out of control, I do have some suggestions on how to help her deal:

1. **Try to nip her extreme appetite in the bud.** Keep snacks handy everywhere—at home, in the car, and in her purse. If you can keep her blood sugar from dropping too low, you'll both be in good shape.
2. **Go to restaurants that serve large portions.** Pregnancy is not a good time for nouveau cuisine or spa food (assuming, of course, that there actually is a good time for them).
3. **Don't shop in bulk for the items she craves.** I know it goes against all logic, but trust me. If you stock up on whatever she craves, she'll lose her affection toward it soon enough, and you'll be stuck with a freezer filled with a dozen packages of bagel dogs.

They Grow Up So Fast . . . Especially in Utero

This second month of gestation has been quite a productive month for your baby. If you can think of your child as a Ding Dong, you can better understand its physical development. The hard outer shell is like your baby's ectoderm layer. This layer will develop into your child's skin, hair, nervous system, and the lining of its nose, ears, and mouth. The moist chocolate cake within will turn into its heart, muscles, bones, blood, and reproductive system. And the creamy white center will soon be its glands, tongue, bladder, and digestive tract. Even at this early stage of its development, your baby's heart has already formed—and it has started to beat. Your little sweetie has somewhat of an oversized head and would probably tip over a lot if born today. He's already sprouted arm buds, leg buds, and rose buds (just making sure you're still with me). Its ears are starting to form but are not able to hear, so if your wife is bugging you about the importance of singing to her belly, you can tell her to keep her pants on a while longer. By the end of this month, your bundle of joy will be about the size of a Corn-Nut.

3

The Third Month

By the time the third month begins, you're well aware of some of the basic problems inflicted upon you by your wife's pregnancy. You've eaten leftover casserole made from leftover stew made from leftover hash. You may have taken on a second job in order to beef up your soon-to-be-depleting bank account. At the very least, you probably have had to cut back on your expenses. Goodbye, French cuisine, hello, French fries. And to top it all off, you're horny as hell.

I'm sure you've heard time and time again that having a baby will change your life forever, but I bet you had no idea this change would happen when your kid isn't much bigger than a finishing nail. The truth is that from the day your wife passes her pregnancy test, your life changes in many unexpected ways. As you're no doubt finding out, some of those ways can be very difficult to handle.

People think that pregnancy is the happiest time in a couple's life. They've seen happy pregnant couples walking the streets hand in hand. But truth be told, the reason the husband is holding his wife's hand is that he's trying to stop her from slapping him across the face.

The secret to enjoying pregnancy is to lower your expectations. If you can think of pregnancy as a nine-month stint at a prisoner-of-war camp (and not a fun one, like on *Hogan's Heroes*), I assure you that you'll endure the process a lot more easily. Another way to survive pregnancy is to prepare for potential surprises so that if they happen, you won't be, you know, surprised. So let's delve into some of the surprises that may take place in month number three, the last month of the first trimester.

What Goodies Await You This Month

The third month of pregnancy can be the most difficult of them all. If your wife is having morning sickness, she's no doubt exhausted from suffering flu-like symptoms for the past two months. But by the end of this first trimester, your wife's erratic hormone levels should start to level off, and some of her ailments, like morning sickness and extreme fatigue, may start to fade. (She'll become exhausted again, but not until the last trimester, when she becomes too big to get any sleep.) Other symptoms, like her mood swings and headaches, may even get worse.

You've been doing a good job taking care of your wife up until now—haven't you?—but she still needs you to keep up the good work. And it might finally start to pay off, because after this month things may get a bit easier. As she lifts her head out of the toilet bowl, her spirits will lift, too, and you'll both feel better knowing that by the end of this month, the risk of miscarriage will be slim and your child has an excellent chance of being a keeper.

But don't slack off now. This month may bring a few surprise ailments that, as of yet, may not have reared their ugly heads.

Her Symptoms and What You Can Do about Them

These are some side effects that can occur during the third month (and at other times), plus what you can do about them.

Nasal Congestion
- **Get her a saline nasal spray** like Ocean Mist.
- **Set up a humidifier.**
- **Get nasal strips** like the football players wear.
- **Rub Vicks VapoRub on her chest.**
- **Give her your pillow** so she can sleep with her head propped up.
- If congestion is severe, **offer her an antihistamine.** Make sure to get her doctor's approval first.

Bloody Nose
- **Set up a humidifier** to help moisten her dry nasal tissues.
- **Get her a saline spray** like Ocean Mist.
- **Have her rub Vaseline around the inside of her nostrils.**

Drooling
- **Get her a bib.**
- **Strap a spittoon** around her neck.
- **Have her stand outside** to water the lawn.

Constipation

- **Make sure that she eats her veggies** (and other fiber-rich food), avoids foods that bind (like cheese and other dairy products), and drinks enough water.
- **Go on a walk with her.**
- **Ask her doctor about changing her brand of prenatal vitamins.** Some cause constipation more than others.
- **If her constipation is severe, have her talk to her doctor** about taking a laxative, a stool softener, or in extreme cases, an enema.
- **Make sure that you use the bathroom before she does.** She may be in there quite a while.

Sympathy Pains

You knew that pregnancy causes your wife to gain weight, but did you also know that it can turn *you* into a potential candidate for *The Biggest Loser*? And that's not all. It seems that men can experience many of the same symptoms that their pregnant wives do. This phenomenon is commonly known as "sympathy pains," but the medical term for it is "couvade syndrome." This must be French for "my butt looks big in these pants, too."

The truth is that it's not that unusual for husbands to gain weight over the nine-month gestation period. I know I did. I had a broad face and a little round belly that shook when I laughed like a bowl full of jelly. And it's no wonder, either. Our cupboards were spilling over with comfort foods for beating morning sickness. And, because of my wife's mood swings, I was in desperate need of comfort myself. In addition, my wife would fix herself a steady stream of snacks, but her craving changed by the time they were ready. So, like a dog, I licked the plate clean. As the months passed, I packed on pounds like Matt Damon for that movie *The Informant*. I never took much notice of it until the day when a stranger asked if she could feel my belly, too.

Sympathy pains aren't restricted to weight gain. In many cases, a father-to-be will experience nausea, heartburn, backache, nightmares, fatigue, and insomnia. Men living with pregnant women also have more headaches and cravings, and they can experience mood swings. Some even feel extreme pain during their wives' labor, but that might just be because their wives are squeezing their hands until their fingers break.

Scientists have several different theories about why men experience sympathy pains. Some experts say that it's because men's hormones change when their partners go through pregnancy. Other experts feel that a man's sympathy pains are a subconscious way for him to try to take the pains away from his wife. Still others say that sympathy pains occur because men are jealous about all the attention, support, and gifts that their wives are being given. No one knows the real reason, but I'll go with the gift thing. I'm not bitter or anything, but after all I went through, a new table saw would have been a very nice gesture.

If you find that your weight gain is getting out of hand and you're in need of some maternity clothes of your own, head on down to your local men's shop. They sell a waistband extension that hooks onto your top pant button and gives you a few extra inches to play around with. If, after the baby's born, you manage to lose your additional weight, keep this extension. It will come in handy during Thanksgiving and Super Bowl Sunday.

Be Afraid, Be Very Afraid

Having a baby can be a scary time for both you and your wife. Your wife is afraid that her water will break all over her new suede pumps. You have fears, too, but don't like to admit them. Instead you keep your fears, like your secret DVD collection, hidden away.

I know you worry that you'll be perceived as a pregnancy sissy and that all the other dads will tease you, but the truth is that all fathers-to-be have these same fears. These are some of the most common:

Your Relationship with Your Wife Might Change

Let me relieve that worry right here and now: It most definitely will. In fact, your relationship with her has already changed. And when the baby comes, it will change even more. But that doesn't mean it'll change for the worse. Although it's not uncommon for a baby to magnify the problems in a marriage that were there before, a new member of the family can create some good changes, too. You and your wife will appreciate each other more and depend on one another like never before. And when you finally have time to be alone, you'll be deliriously happy. This may have less to do with how much you love being together, and more to do with how much you love being away from the house and the screaming kid. Either way, you'll be deliriously happy.

You Won't Be Able to Protect Your Family

It's been ingrained in your DNA that you are the protector of the house. Even at this point of the pregnancy, you're more aware of your wife's safety than ever before. When you walk with her down the street, you're aware of every high curb she may stumble upon, or any passerby who might collide with her belly. You're like her own personal NORAD permanently set at DEFCON Five. I know of more than one new father who bought a gun to keep his family safe. Me, I just put some new batteries in the smoke detectors and called it a day.

You Won't Be Able to Provide for the Baby

No matter what tax bracket he's in, every man worries about the costs of raising a child. Of course, the stress factor is made more intense if you're having trouble making ends meet already with just the two of you. Maybe you want to have one of you stay home with the baby. You'll have to learn how to live on one paycheck. But, along with the doctor bills and endless diaper purchases, you can find some financial advantages to having a baby as well (hello, tax deduction!).

You Won't Handle Childbirth Well

Maybe you're afraid that being in the delivery room will prove to be a bit scary for you. You can barely handle seeing the juices flow from a rare piece of steak, let alone watch a baby being born. Between your wife screaming and the constant pouring of bodily fluids, you'll feel like you're at a crime scene. The truth is that it really may be hard to take. If this is the case, talk to your wife. I doubt that she'll want you in the delivery room if you're going to be a hindrance and take away any attention from where it belongs—completely on her and the baby. And I know that her doctor will agree.

The Baby Your Wife Is Carrying Isn't Yours

Admit it. The thought has crossed your mind (and if it didn't before, it certainly will now—sorry). You've heard stories. You've watched soap opera commercials. You know it's been known to happen. I admit that I had this fear myself, and it continued for years. When we went in for our amniocentesis, our genetic counselor told us that since my wife and I both have green eyes, our child would, too. So when our daughter was born with blue eyes, I panicked. Then I was told that all babies had blue eyes, so I went with it for a while. After two years they remained blue, though, and my patience ran thin. I confronted my wife about my suspicion and she was horribly insulted. Soon afterward, my daughter's eyes finally changed color. Either I spoke too soon, or my wife wakes up early each morning and puts colored contacts in our daughter's eyes. I try not to think about it anymore.

Death

You may have the fear that your wife will die during childbirth. Put that to rest. The truth is, there has never been a safer time to give birth. Your wife has a much greater chance of being killed on the way to the hospital than dying in childbirth (now doesn't that make you feel more at ease?) You may also worry about your child's death. Maybe you fear that your wife will miscarry or that your child will be born with some debilitating disease. You may even fear your own death and realize how important it is for you to eat all your veggies from now on. There's nothing like bringing a new life into the world to make you start worrying about having it taken away.

These are but a handful of fears. Don't worry if you have
several others that I didn't mention. Just realize that pregnancy is an emotional time and that it tends to make you
freak out. The best way that I found to relieve my fears was
to visit a toy store. I breathed a big sigh of relief when I saw
how much fun having a kid would actually be. After seeing
aisles laden with Slinkies, red wagons, pogo sticks, and Hot
Wheels, I not only left the store more relaxed about my fears,
but I also left with a bag full of fun ways to kill time until
the kid showed up.

Headache, Anyone?

Headaches are one of those lesser-known pregnancy side
effects that no one ever tells you about. And I'm not talking
about the headaches that your wife gets. I'm talking about
the ones she inflicts on you. The reason that your wife has so
much head pain is because of her skyrocketing hormone levels, and her constant fatigue, hunger, and stress. The reason
for your pain is that you live with her.

The way you both treat your headaches might differ, too.
All you need to do is take two aspirin and say goodbye to
pain. But for your wife, things can get more complicated. To
begin with, not all obstetricians approve of pregnant women
taking pain relievers. They're purists and don't want to take
even the most minuscule risk of harming the baby. And
even if your wife's doctor okays the pills, your wife may be
reluctant. She may be a purist, too, and would never forgive
herself if she hurt even one hair on his tiny, yet oversized
little head.

My wife tried to take the more natural approach to pain relief through using things such as cold compresses and aromatherapy candles. I, on the other hand, would gently try to convince her to take the Tylenol that her doctor approved—actually, I would beg and plead. Nature is fine for a weekend at Yosemite, but for pain, I'd go with the strong stuff anytime. But she refused and suffered in silence, or at least that noisy kind of silence where she whined and complained for hours on end. During her headaches, my wife felt an odd connection to Laura Ingalls from *Little House on the Prairie*. She'd go on and on about how poor little Laura must have suffered too because there wasn't any Tylenol back in her day. Forget the fact that there wasn't any central heat or indoor plumbing—let's feel bad that little Laura didn't have any gelcaps.

Eventually, my wife gave in. I'm not sure if it was because of the lingering pain or my constant begging, but my wife finally started using Tylenol. She felt better, I felt better, and, because my wife had so many headaches, the shareholders of Tylenol felt better, too.

If you and your wife are suffering from headaches, head them off at the pass. Try to help her get a good night's sleep, make sure that she eats small meals throughout the day to keep her blood sugar up, and reduce her stress level in whatever ways you can. If your wife still has headaches and refuses to take her doctor-approved pain reliever, you can try some of the more natural approaches described in Chapter 2, in the section titled "Her Symptoms and What You Can Do about Them." But no matter what you do, don't let her watch any television shows that are set during the frontier era, or at any time before people had ever heard of the word "acetaminophen."

Un-Beauty Marks

Up until now, we've only discussed the physical changes that occur on the inside of your wife's body. But many changes may take place on the outside as well. As with most of her other ailments, these too are caused by, you guessed it, hormones (you're getting pretty good at this pregnancy thing!). And, just like the other ailments, most will go away after your tax write-off is born.

Even though you're helpless to change them, you should be aware of these effects because they can be downright scary. I can handle a lot of gross things. I've held things in my hands that only surgeons and Jeffrey Dahmer have held. Even though my tolerance for gross is high, I wasn't prepared for some of the physical changes that took place in my wife's body. Because of this, I want to warn you about some upcoming "unattractions." This way you won't be so surprised, and you can have a moment to either regain your thoughts or search the house for a blindfold.

Because some changes arrive later than others, I've listed them like the actors in many movies, in the order of their appearance. So let me introduce you to the cast of characters:

1. **From the beginning, your wife's nipples will change.** They will grow larger, darker, and become pointier as her body prepares to breastfeed. The areola (the circular area around the nipple) will darken and become bigger, giving your almost colorblind newborn a target to aim for. Her areolas will also get lumpier and tend to pucker.

2. **Her vaginal area may look different.** It may get darker throughout her pregnancy and become more swollen as it becomes engorged with blood. Her discharge

will get thicker and the whole area may have a different scent and taste.

3. **You may be able to see your wife's veins and arteries through her skin.** It's as if her skin was suddenly replaced by Saran Wrap. She may also develop more moles and spider veins.

4. **Because of the increase in the amount of male hormones** (yup, she has them, too), **she may grow darker and thicker facial and chest hair.** It seems that pregnancy is Mother Nature's form of Rogaine.

5. **Her hands and feet may change color.** Her palms may redden and her feet may develop a bluish tinge.

6. **She may develop an extra nipple on her chest.** Let me say that again just in case, like me, you didn't believe it the first time you read it: Your wife may develop an extra nipple on her chest. This is actually a common malformation that many people are born with. It can pass unnoticed (it may resemble a bump or a mole) until the hormones of pregnancy get a hold of it, and then it becomes more obvious. If your wife's boobs are still sore, you may get lucky and have a chance to fondle this extra one.

7. **Her nails will thicken and grow longer than ever before.** Although this may make for a nice back scratch from time to time, the real purpose of these claws is to better inflict pain on you during delivery.

8. **She may grow extra flaps of skin called skin tags on high-friction skin areas like her bra line and underarms.**

9. **A dark line may appear on your wife's stomach,** starting at her bellybutton and traveling down to her crotch.

10. **As the skin on your wife's body stretches, you may notice lines that span across her skin.** These are those stretch marks you've heard so much about. This usually hap-

pens around her breasts and stomach. Some lotions promise to erase these lines, but they can't.

11. **Your wife may get PUPPP**—not the cute things that grow up to be man's best friend, but the gross thing that's basically a rash that develops in your wife's stretch marks as well as on her thighs, butt, and arms.

12. **Her bellybutton may pop out like a turkey timer.** Unfortunately, unlike with the timer, this is not a sign that your little gobbler is done and is now ready to come out of the oven.

13. **Her breasts may leak a thick yellow substance called "colostrum."** To gross you out even more (as if that's possible), they may even leak a drop or two of blood. Now if that isn't scary, I don't know what is.

As I stated, these "un-beauty" marks usually disappear after delivery. And if they don't, there's usually some overpriced specialist who can get rid of anything that's left over. I recommend that you don't take this route until after all of your children are born, unless you enjoy throwing your hard-earned money away.

How to Sleep with a Jackhammer

Yet another annoying side effect of pregnancy is that your wife's nasal tissues are drier than Steven Wright's sense of humor. Because of this, she must suffer through her constant congestion. You, on the other hand, must suffer through her constant snoring. And let me tell you, a pregnancy snore ain't pretty. It's loud and it's constant. It's like sleeping next to someone who's grinding up the starter on an old Buick.

This pregnancy snore is frustrating to deal with. The first and most obvious reason why is that it keeps you up all night. Just when you're finally able to doze off, a burst of construction noise goes off at the next pillow. And second, unlike when you snore, you can't just give your spouse a poke and have her roll over. As you've probably figured out by now, sleep is very important to a pregnant woman, and disturbing such sleep may result in your taking a more permanent night's residence on the sofa. Besides, rolling over is no easy task for a pregnant woman without the help of an earth mover.

The reason that sleep is such a big issue for your wife is that getting any of it can be quite a big challenge. She may have a backache or a leg cramp or heartburn or any number of conditions that make sleeping difficult. Later on, her belly will be so large that she isn't able to lie on her stomach anymore, and she's not allowed to sleep on her back since doing so may restrict the blood flow to the baby. So she's forced to sleep on her side and will wake up in a panic if she accidentally rolls over.

Some wives may feel guilty about their snoring and apologize. But not my wife. For her it provided an enormous sense of revenge because I myself was a snorer. Her congestion seemed to even up the snoring scorecard, and keeping me up nights made her want to be pregnant year-round.

If you need to get some beauty rest, there are some things that you can try to silence her:

1. **Use earplugs.** Look on the back of the package for the highest noise reduction rating.
2. **Have your wife spray a couple of drops of saline spray in her nose.** We found Ocean Mist worked best.

3. **Have your wife sleep with her head elevated.** If she has heartburn, this will help take off some of the heat as well.
4. **Rub a menthol rub (like Vicks) on her chest.** Not only will you get a better night's sleep, but you'll get a cheap thrill.
5. **Sleep with a pillow over your head.** This trick will also come in handy after the baby's born so that you won't hear it crying and your wife will have to get up instead of you.
6. **Use a humidifier in the room to reduce her congestion and thus her snoring.** If the humidifier is loud enough, it may even drown out the sound of her snoring.
7. **Have her wear the kind of nasal strips that the football players do.** Not only should this reduce her decibel level, but it should take away some of your unfulfilled sexual desire.

The snoring won't go on forever. After your baby is born, your wife's snoring should stop. My wife's did. And coincidentally, so did mine. But for me, it had less to do with my daughter's birth than the fact that I underwent three nasal surgeries. Between my wife having to wake up constantly with the new baby and with my frequent snoring, she became incredibly bitchy . . . uh, I mean, sleep-deprived. So I had most of my face removed in order to keep peace in the house.

Your Wife Is One Big Baby

When they tell you that pregnancy can transform a woman into a glowing, sexy, voluptuous creature full of stamina and sexual desire, they often fail to mention the ways it can turn her into a big baby. Instead of acting like a temptress, she'll act more like a toddler. Here are some of the changes you need to man up for:

1. **She doesn't drink.** It used to be that you and your wife would go out at night, toss back a few, and dance the night away. But now the only drink your wife tosses back is a cold glass of moo-juice. Although you understand why she does it and know it's best for the baby, it gets rather tiresome to drink alone.

2. **She goes to bed early.** Gone are the nights when you two would cozy up together on the sofa, light a fire, and talk the night away (okay, that went away after the first month of dating). Now your wife gets so tired at the end of the day—hell, who am I kidding, by afternoon—that it's just you on the couch. Although this may seem boring, you should focus on the positive. You can finally have unchallenged control of the remote.

3. **She doesn't have sex.** They say that when you get married your sex life changes, but never in the history of your marriage will it change as fast as when you conceive. Although it takes sex to have a baby, it takes the baby to take it away.

4. **She doesn't smoke.** If you both were smokers before the pregnancy, you may miss this part most of all. Not only does your wife have to stop, but she's going to nag you about stopping, too. She won't even let you smoke around her or within a two-mile radius. And that holds true for anyone else. With her superhuman

sense of smell, she can track down a smoker and stomp all over his butt.

Once you start thinking of your wife as a baby instead of a broad, you'll notice other similarities as well. She burps constantly. She farts without shame. She has tantrums and crying jags. And, if she has morning sickness, she eats food like mashed potatoes, milkshakes, and mac-and-cheese, and then projectile vomits them away. I know it's hard to live with a woman-child, but there is one advantage to it. For the next nine months, you'll never be without a designated driver.

Job Insecurity

Expecting a baby doesn't just mean having a more difficult home life; it can mean having a more difficult work life as well. It seems that when you've created a new life, the importance of little things like earning a living just doesn't carry the same weight anymore. You tend to lose your ambition and are quite content to stay put on your rung of the corporate ladder.

The catch is that, now more than ever, you should want to do a good job. You know how vital a weekly paycheck is from now on and your boss may not like your new relaxed approach. It's hard to focus on the Blair account when you're posting your recent ultrasound photo on Facebook. It's tough finding time for your conference call when you're on the phone with your wife, who rambles on about a new hemorrhoid.

Your job will become even more challenging if you hold a managerial position in which you need to motivate workers. You can't seem to raise your voice anymore if a worker hasn't filled his daily quota of making plastic forks. You know that deep down in the scheme of things, it isn't all that important (except for those eating potato salad at a picnic).

No matter what your job title, whether you're a blue-collar or white-collar worker, you can expect your work life to change. Sometimes it seems that starting a new life may just be ending your career.

This same situation holds true for your wife. Like you, she'll be faced with more challenges and job stresses, and in addition, she'll have to pee every twenty minutes. That's why it's a good idea for both of you to tell your bosses about the pregnancy before you tell anyone else. Normally I recommend that you wait three months before you blab about the good news so that you're out of the miscarriage woods. But when it comes to the boss, I think that you should call him as soon as you see the two blue lines. Keeping your job is very important right now. You have teethers to buy, pacifiers to stock up on. And braces to save up for, made necessary by the teethers and pacifiers. If you decide not to tell your boss about the upcoming happy event the same day you find out yourself, make sure that you do so just as soon as you feel comfortable and confident enough with the pregnancy.

There may be a part of you that's tempted to wait as long as you can. You may be afraid that once your boss finds out that your wife is expecting, he'll know that you're going to slack off more. But tell him anyway. Sure, right now you may slack off a bit and rush home early to spend more time with your wife, but in the end, he'll come out ahead. Way ahead. Even though work may not be such a priority right now, after the baby's born, you'll be making up the lost hours big time. Not because you'll get your ambition back, but because you'll want to get away from the screaming, exhausted, laundry-ridden poopfest that you once called home. And because your wife will be so sleep-deprived and yell at you so much, you'll take that anger to work and scream at that fork guy even more, and he'll produce more forks than he ever did before.

Practice, Practice, Practice

Other than actually growing the child, pregnancy enables you to get used to the way your life will be after delivery. During pregnancy, you'll face a lot of the same types of challenges that you'll encounter once baby makes three. Consider pregnancy a dress rehearsal for the big show.

Although these lessons may be difficult to learn, consider yourself lucky. Parents of adopted babies may not have as easy a time getting used to life with a newborn. They didn't have the advantage of preparing for nine long months to make the transition a smooth one. They had to hit the ground running.

Sometimes you won't even realize that you're learning anything at all. Although some of the ways that you're being prepared for parenthood are apparent, others are more subtle in nature. But believe me, during this gestational phase you're learning the skills needed to cope as a new parent. Let's take a look at what some of the preparations are:

Dress Rehearsal versus Opening Day

Life While Pregnant	Life After Delivery
You can't sleep because your wife is restless	You can't sleep because your baby cries
You constantly have to change poopy kitty litter	You constantly have to change poopy diapers
You put your wife's needs above your own	You put your baby's needs above your own
You live with a hormonal, bitchy wife	You live with a sleep-deprived, hormonal, bitchy wife
Your wife wants to eat everything off your plate	Your child throws everything off your plate
Your doctor tests you for possible genetic diseases	Your child tests your patience
You go to bed early because your wife's so exhausted	You go to bed early because you're so exhausted
You pass on buying a new leather jacket because your wife needs maternity clothes	You pass on buying a leather jacket because your kid needs new baby clothes
You live with a gassy wife	You live with a gassy baby
You live with a woman obsessed with her poops	You live with a woman obsessed with her baby's poops
Your wife doesn't want to have sex	Your wife still doesn't want to have sex

These are only a handful of ways that Mother Nature's preparing you for the adjustments of parenthood. By the time that your wife huffs and puffs and blows your kid out, you'll be expertly accustomed to the demands of parenthood because, as you know, practice makes perfect.

They Grow Up So Fast ... Especially in Utero

This month your baby has performed an amazing accomplishment: It's taken its first whiz! I know it sounds strange, but from now on your kid will pee as freely in its amniotic fluid as you do in your own backyard. It's also not an "it" any more, for the baby's genitals are well on their way to being formed. In fact, if your child is a boy you can actually make out his tiny little package on an ultrasound. Your baby's intestines are formed, but they're on the outside of its body, which could make finding a prom date quite a challenge. Luckily this problem should rectify itself by the following month, leaving him plenty of time before he has to rent his powder blue tuxedo. In case you're wondering, your baby weighs about as much as a golf tee.

4

The Fourth Month

Break out the champagne! The fourth month of pregnancy is definitely a time for celebration. No, wait, put the champagne away; your wife can't have any. But celebrate anyway: If you've made it this far, your baby has a more than 90 percent chance of going the distance. Statistics also show that once you get past this crucial trimester, your wife has a less than 3 percent chance of killing you. So raise a glass of sparkling apple cider and make a toast to your good fortune.

You should savor this toast while it lasts because the celebration may not continue very long. Although your wife's morning sickness should dissipate, her mood swings are still in full force. You spend your day apologizing for things you did or didn't do in an attempt to atone. You've come to realize that pregnancy means always having to say you're sorry.

Pregnant women don't mean to be this way. You have to realize that, just like you, your wife is going through her own pregnancy awakening. She's shocked and frustrated that her joyous days of pregnancy aren't turning out to be so joyous after all. She's always dreamed of holding a baby in her arms, but she's now realizing that it's not that great to hold one in her belly. She may be experiencing more discomfort than she bargained for. Or she may be realizing that she won't be like one of those gorgeous pregnant celebrities who gain as much weight during their whole nine months as she just did over this past three-day weekend.

The good news is that most women find the second trimester the easiest to deal with. Some women say that it fills them with an endless supply of energy. For my wife, it just filled her with an endless supply of gas.

What Goodies Await You This Month

I know you've done a lot of things to make your wife more comfortable during the first trimester. You've rubbed Vicks on her chest, you've fed her crackers, and you've held her head while she puked. But now not only are you one-third done with pregnancy, you're one-third done with the pregnancy ailments!

You can expect this second trimester to be the best one of the bunch. It's the eye of the pregnancy hurricane. Your wife is happy because her morning sickness is over. She can finally put on a bra without tearing up, and most important, she finally has a baby bump! Other people can tell that she's pregnant and not just letting herself go. But in between her smiles, she still may have some more challenges to face, and you, her lapdog of pregnancy, will have to face them right along with her.

Her Symptoms and What You Can Do about Them

During the second trimester, she may experience a few new symptoms. Here are some pointers to help her deal with them.

Bloody Gums

There's really nothing you can do to stop them from bleeding. But since they don't hurt her, she shouldn't hurt you either. Make sure that she continues to go for her dental checkups, since pregnancy can be very taxing on her gums. The dentist should know about her condition, because x-rays and medication should be avoided.

Vaginal Discharge

You may notice that your wife has a thicker discharge than before. There's nothing you can do to stop this, either, and it shouldn't cause your wife so much discomfort that she will complain to you about it (see, I told you this month was going to be one of the easier ones). Be prepared, though. She may send you out to the drugstore to stock up on panty shields!

Sex in the Second Trimester

Because of her nausea, constipation, spotting, and mood swings, you may be thinking that your sex life is officially over. But this may be the month that your fat lady finally sings! Or at least moans and groans with pleasure—if you play your cards right.

Your wife is probably feeling better and has more energy. Between her new outlook on life, her higher levels of male hormones, and her engorged body parts, she's capable of having the greatest sex of her life.

If you're fortunate enough to experience this erotic free-for-all, enjoy it while it lasts. For this new sexual awakening may soon drift into a coma and stay that way until . . . well, let's just say my daughter is about to start kindergarten and

I'm still waiting for it to come back. But for now you can expect to have more sex than ever before, and it will be hotter than the porn stuff you watched at the fertility clinic. My wife felt that her body wasn't hers anymore, and it must have belonged to a sex maniac because it was always raring to go.

On the other hand, this second trimester may be just as barren as the one before it. Many men claim that there wasn't much action during the middle part of pregnancy. They're convinced that the second-trimester horniness is just an urban legend. The truth is that not all women become sex kittens. Some women still aren't out of their hormone surge yet. Some may have spotted after first-trimester sex and are too afraid to try it again. Other women have issues to deal with about being a mother and how mothers should behave. If any of this is true, maybe you can convince your wife to talk to her doctor. He may be able to alleviate her multiple fears by educating her about her chances of multiple orgasms.

Although some pregnant women lose their libido during pregnancy, they aren't always the ones responsible for the lack of action in the sack. It's not uncommon for a man to have a lower sex drive during his wife's pregnancy. Some are afraid of hurting the baby or think their penis will somehow break the amniotic sac that holds the baby. Others, particularly those who were surprised by the pregnancy, may be turned off. They weren't ready for kids, and, even though they know that having sex isn't going to make their wives any more pregnant, they still don't have a desire. Others just aren't turned on by their pregnant wives' physiques. A guy in this situation would never admit it (at least not out loud), but the woman next to him in bed is heavier, more demanding, angrier, and more flatulent than the one he said "I do" to.

I sincerely hope that your second trimester is one filled with lust, heat, and little obligatory foreplay. If it is, consider yourself lucky and say a silent prayer for the frustrated men all over the world who are singing the blues.

Two Magic Words

Just as the phrase "abracadabra" can enable a magician to pull a rabbit out of his hat, there's a magical phrase that men with expectant wives should know. It, too, has been used throughout history to perform a trick—in this case, the trick of keeping their pregnant woman happy. This magical phrase consists of two simple yet very potent words: "Yes, dear."

Right now, your wife is on the hormonal roller-coaster ride from hell, and, unfortunately, that safety bar has you locked in place right beside her. At times you'll be cruising along just fine and then suddenly, life will throw you into a sharp curve and your wife will become a screaming lunatic. She doesn't mean to be. She isn't even aware of it most of the time. But suddenly, and without much provocation, you're the one that'll be screaming for dear life.

That's where the magic of "Yes, dear" comes into play. It's the hocus-pocus of pregnancy. I suggest that you memorize this magic duo and practice until saying it becomes second nature. You'll transform your wife's pinched and scowling face into the smiling, water-retaining one that you've grown to love.

You may have learned how to be somewhat of a magician already. God knows that you're not a novice in the arena of womanly hormones. You've been aware of them ever since the time you were a little boy, and you noticed that every twenty-eight days your dad would walk around wearing a hardhat. I'm sure that by now you have a few tricks up your sleeves to help deal with them.

If you're the kind of person who freezes under pressure, there are some backup expressions that possess the same magical quality. In a pinch, you can try a simple variation, like "Anything you say, dear" or "You know best" or "Whatever you think, hon." Just keep as far as possible from any expressions like "You're wrong" or "That's crazy" or "You must be out of your fat-ass freakin' mind."

Unfortunately, even though the hormones start to stabilize after the first three months, you still can't get off the ride—this roller coaster won't come to a complete stop until years after the baby is born. So keep this magical phrase handy. No, it won't enable you to pull money out from an unsuspecting ear, but it will help you take your foot out of your mouth, which is quite a good trick in itself.

Pregnancy Tests for You

Since the day your wife first went to the OB, she's had to endure many tests. She's peed in cups, donated blood to countless tubes, and had her cervix swabbed. Up until now you've gotten off pretty easy. But your wife may not be the only one who is going to get poked and prodded during the pregnancy process (try saying that three times fast). Even though you're not the one carrying the baby (no matter how much your wife wants you to), you may still have to undergo some tests of your own.

The number of tests and the types that may be performed will pretty much depend on your ethnic origin. If your ancestors were Eastern European Jews, you can expect a test for Tay-Sachs disease. If you're African-American, it's a test for sickle cell for you. Even if you're from the planet Mars, you'll probably have to undergo some type of test (more likely a psychological test if you say you're from Mars). That's because many genetic conditions can only be passed on to your kid if both you and your wife carry the gene.

For instance, my wife is Jewish so she was tested for Tay-Sachs, since she has a small, but possible, chance of carrying the gene. But my non-Jewish family has been living in the tiny town of Humansville, Missouri, for several generations. The doctors have a greater chance of finding a monkey up my butt than the Tay-Sachs gene, but I still had to be tested.

Even if you have to undergo a genetic evaluation, all in all, your involvement in the pregnancy test arena isn't such a big deal. And you'd better not complain about it to your wife. By the time she delivers, she'll have undergone many tests, some of which can take up to three hours. So bite the bullet and be strong, and give thanks yet one more time to Mother Nature for not giving you a female reproductive system.

Why It's Good to Be Girly (for a While)

Men aren't emotional creatures. We don't like to sit around for hours drinking flavored coffee and sharing our innermost thoughts. It's not in our nature. But you put two women together and within five minutes they know the intimate details about each other's menstrual flow. Guys aren't like that. Never have been. Never will be. Except when their wives are expecting.

Because of some anomaly of nature, something happens to a man when he lives with a pregnant woman. While your wife's pregnancy is causing her to grow more facial and chest hair, it's bringing out your feminine side. You now find that you open up to complete strangers. For years you've worked with Stan in accounting without uttering more than an occasional hello. But now that his wife is pregnant as well, neither of you can shut up. Instead of your usual guy-to-guy conversations, you now focus on different things:

Expressing Your Feminine Side

Your Old Conversation	Your New Conversation
Tiger's incredible golf swing	Your wife's incredible mood swing
If the Kings were able to score last night	If you were able to score last night
The new German-engineered four-wheel-drive sports car	The new German-engineered four-wheel-drive stroller
Your golf handicap	Your sperm count
Your thinning hair	Your wife's thickening nipple hair

You can't stop yourself from doing it. You tell Stan things that you never told your closest buddy. That's because Stan doesn't laugh at you when you admit that you sang to the belly last night. He understands when you tell him your wife threw a pizza at you last night because you forgot to order extra cheese. He understands the pregnancy lingo like "Braxton-Hicks" and "Diaper Genie," so you don't have to keep explaining yourself like you're forced to do with your nonpregnant friends. Stan understands you and, oddly enough, you both suddenly understand women. Finally, after years of struggle, you understand how the opposite sex thinks. You get how the bonding and sharing with another person can make you feel accepted and understood. Suddenly you feel a surge of estrogen and can finally comprehend why your wife feels the need to clean up before the housekeeper comes.

But just like with your wife's superhuman sense of smell, your girly side won't last either. Once your toddler is in tow it may pop out from time to time, but only when you meet a father with a child the exact same age and sex as your own. By then, though, you'll be so sleep-deprived that you won't have the energy to do much talking.

How to Travel with a Pregnant Woman

In some ways, traveling during pregnancy is a good thing. It gets you out of the house and can be a great way to get some romance back into your marriage. By now it's suffered some of the slings and arrows of outrageous frustration that hormones and sleep deprivation can bring, and it's time to reconnect. Away from home, your wife will be more relaxed. She'll take her mind off of her pregnancy ailments, and she will be farther away from the kitchen knives that scare you so. It also may be your last traveling hurrah. Once Junior makes his appearance, the only places you'll frequent are theme parks and restaurants that give out crayons.

Traveling with a pregnant woman can be stressful. At times you'll feel like the only place you're going is to hell and back. Even though traveling during pregnancy may have many advantages, there are some things that you should be aware of before you put the pedal to the metal.

Car Travel

1. **If your destination isn't that far away, plan on driving there.** But even if the road is free of potholes, you should still expect some bumps inside the car. First of all, no matter what your speed, your wife will insist that you're driving too fast. It seems that her maternal instinct is in full gear. Even if you don't agree with her, slow down. Let's just say that if an old lady in a Falcon passes you, you know that you're going at just the right speed.

2. **Expect that your wife will be the navigator.** She may insist you travel a route that you never knew existed before. It may be the slow way. It may be the really slow way. But don't fight her, just do it. She has hormones and knows how to use them.

3. **If your wife is having morning sickness,** be sure to travel with a good supply of plastic bags and crackers in your glove compartment.

4. **Allow plenty of extra time for pee breaks, leg cramps, and to stretch out backaches and sciatica pain.** The general rule of thumb is to leave the day before you actually need to be there.

5. **If your wife is feeling nauseated,** it's not only important to slow down going into a curve, it's also important to slow down inside of it, and when you leave it as well.

6. **If the pressure is too much for you, let your wife drive.** Keep in mind that she may be more forgetful now

that she's pregnant, and won't pay as close attention to the road. She may miss an exit or hit a small woodland creature. But don't utter a word to upset her. Her lungs have more horsepower than the engine.

Airplane Travel

1. **If you're traveling by air, bring along some snacks to nibble on throughout the trip.** Because of budget restraints, many airlines have canceled their in-flight meal service and now just scatter some hay throughout the aisles for the herd of passengers to graze from.

2. **It's a good idea to note where the restrooms are located before you take off, in case of morning sickness or an emergency pee break.** Also, if any meals are served, have your wife try to pee beforehand. Afterward the lines tend to back up. In an emergency, use the restroom at the back of the plane. They're more likely to be vacant.

3. **If your wife is past her seventh month, she won't be able to fly.** You may think that this rule was made because there won't be enough airplane food to feed her, but it's actually because the airlines don't want to pick up any additional travelers midflight.

4. **By far the best part about traveling with a pregnant woman is that some airlines let you board early.** There's nothing that makes you feel more like a celebrity than marching to the front of the long airport line and having the ropes open up for you to pass through.

Bus or Train

1. **The best form of travel is bus or train, because in both situations neither of you is driving.** It's highly unlikely, although still possible, that your wife will yell at the conductor for going too fast, or blame the bus driver for going the wrong way.

2. **Another excellent reason for choosing these modes of transportation is that there are other travelers around, so your wife is less likely to raise her voice.** I'm not saying that she won't do it. We both know that she certainly has the capacity to do so, but the chances are greatly reduced.

How to Exercise for Two

Your wife knows that she should exercise, but because of her fatigue, nausea, backache, sore boobs, and her ever-changing center of gravity, she finds that just getting into her maternity exercise gear is enough of a workout.

But exercise really is just what the doctor ordered. It's good for your wife's circulatory system and may prevent varicose veins and hemorrhoids. It increases her endurance level, which will come in handy for the hours of pushing during labor. It also helps keep her weight gain to a minimum, which may allow her to get back into her pre-pregnancy jeans faster. Although this last part may not help out with her pregnancy, it certainly doesn't hurt.

That's not to say that she should overexert herself. Unless your wife was used to doing workouts before she got pregnant, now is not the time for her to take up any rigorous exercise regime or a high-risk sport. As always, a quick consult with the doctor can't hurt. You'll undoubtedly learn that there are many forms of exercise she can do. But that doesn't mean she has to do them alone.

You can be the best motivator that she has to push her tush in gear. And, if you've packed on a few extra sympathy pounds, you need to push your tush as well. Here are a few ways that you both can get physical:

1. **Walking:** A brisk twenty-minute walk will do wonders for her energy level. She should never walk so fast that it's difficult for her to bark out orders without getting winded.
2. **Swimming:** Most pregnant women love to swim because it takes the baby's weight off their stomach. It's also quite safe, because their boobs are so big and buoyant that there's little chance of drowning.
3. **Prenatal yoga:** My wife loved it because it cured her sciatica and let her bond with other preggos.

How Your Wife Needs You to Behave

Most people say that their second pregnancy experience was easier than their first. I'm sure this is because by time the second one comes along, the husband knows his place in the pregnancy food chain.

I wish someone had told me these rules from the start. I'm not saying it would have made my pregnancy experience any more enjoyable, but it sure would have made it quieter.

My Rules of Pregnancy

1. **Abstain from the same things that your wife has to abstain from.** If she can't have a glass of wine, you can't either. If she can't have too much caffeine, neither should you. I know it might be a hard thing to do, but if you can, your wife will think of you as a team player and that will make her happy. Of course, as soon as she's out of the room or you're out of the house, all bets are off.

2. **Give your wife plenty of unexpected kisses,** and don't forget to kiss her ass on a daily basis.

3. **Write her a love letter from time to time and leave it somewhere for her to find later.** This way she knows that you love her and she has no chance of yelling at you on the spot, just in case you write something that may set her off.

4. **Listen to her complain but don't complain back.** In this case, it's definitely better to receive than to give.

5. **Kiss her belly hello and goodbye as you come and go.** You may feel silly, but it will make your wife think that you're trying to connect with the baby.

6. **Don't ever look at or talk about another woman.** It doesn't matter if she's ugly, married, or a member of your own family. This behavior is guaranteed to make your wife jealous.

7. **Reassure your wife by telling her that she's going to be a great mom.** Buy her a Mother's Day present on Mother's Day even if your baby isn't born yet.

8. **Rub her feet no matter how stinky they are.**

9. **At night, give her your pillow to put between her legs for support.** You may feel better yourself knowing that at least something of yours is in there.

10. **When you go out to a store or the mall together,** drop her off in front and park the car yourself so she doesn't have to walk far.

11. **Tell her how little weight she's gained and that she doesn't even look pregnant from behind.** Don't tell her that it's because her behind is so huge that it's blocking any possible view of her stomach.

12. **Don't change anything!** Pregnant women don't seem to like change. They, like the babies that they're carrying, find comfort in consistency and repetition.

In general, until the baby is born, you need to act like the caring, loving, and compassionate man that your mother tried so hard to raise. I hope that you can learn from my mistakes. If I can help even one father-to-be, then it will have made my nights of sleeping on the sofa well worth it.

The Difference Between Boys and Girls

Your father was wrong when he told you about the birds and bees. He explained about differences between the sexes, the innie parts and the outtie ones, and the various body hair that grows in between. But it seems that Pop left out one big difference. And this difference comes into play when a man is told that he's going to be a father.

When a girl finds out that she's expecting, she'll worry about whether she'll be a good mother, how her relationship with her husband will change, and if she'll ever have the same body. A boy, on the other hand, will focus on one main subject: How can we afford this thing? The financial aspect of going forth and multiplying can send him to the brink of despair.

A boy's financial concern is broken down into two distinct parts: A) Will I be able to make enough money to support my family, and B) how much does it cost to have a kid anyway?

I can't help you with the first part because I don't know anything about your earning potential, your ambition, or how many wealthy people you've befriended in order to be put in their wills. But I may be of some assistance in the second part. In this section of the book, I'll discuss the expenses associated with your baby while it's still inside your wife. Later on, I'll break down the expenses when the baby is on the outside.

My list of expenses is based on a healthy nine-month pregnancy and delivery. If your wife has any problems that require prolonged bed rest that will keep her from working, or physical conditions like toxemia or placenta previa that may make additional medical intervention necessary, your list may be different.

The major expense at this stage will be the medical costs. Your health insurance should cover a good portion of the expenses, but call the company now to get an estimate of your share so there won't be any surprises down the road.

The following is a cost breakdown chart so that you can estimate your own expenses. Specific amounts can vary greatly depending on where you live, what type of insurance you have, and your particular circumstances. You can get approximate costs from surfing the web, visiting a baby store, and asking another "pregnant" male what he had to pay.

Cost Chart

Expense	Cost Estimate
Doctor office visits (a minimum of twelve)	
Ultrasounds (two on average)	
Genetic testing	
Lab work (about five tests may be needed)	
Maternity clothes (include work-related, casual, and seasonal clothing; add a premium if your wife is a clotheshorse)	
Cell phones	
Lamaze or other birthing class	
Baby CPR class	
Baby furniture (crib, changing table, bassinet)	
Car seat (you'll need this to take the kid home from the hospital)	
New shoes for your wife's constantly spreading feet	
Extra food to satisfy her cravings (especially the extra protein that she's craving)	
A gift to give your wife the day that your baby is born (optional, but will forever be mentioned if you don't have one)	
Parking at the doctor's office (ours cost $12 a pop)	
Giant bottles of Tums every week for her heartburn	
Baby announcements	
Higher air conditioning bill because your wife will be so hot all the time	
Takeout meals because your wife will be too tired to cook	
European stretch mark prevention creams that get rid of nothing but your money	
Nine months' worth of panty shields	
Dozens of pregnancy and baby-naming books	
Hospital delivery costs	
OB delivery cost	
	Total:

Yes, I know that you could build a five-bedroom house for the same cost as building a baby, but you can find some ways to cut back on expenses. I'll discuss these various ways with you in Chapter 6, in the section called "Saving a Few Bucks." Maybe with the money you save, you can one day think about getting your child something really nice, like a sibling.

They Grow Up So Fast . . . Especially in Utero

Your baby has grown a lot this month. In fact, by the end of this fourth month it will have quadrupled in size. Although you probably find this to be an impossible feat, your baby is gaining weight at a faster rate than your wife! Your baby can now perform difficult tasks like blinking, sucking, and swallowing. It can move its eyes and is already practicing rolling them for when it becomes a teenager and you say something dumb. Speaking of moving, your baby's doing a lot of it these days. A few moms can even feel their babies moving toward the end of the month. You, on the other hand, will have to wait a while longer, until your kid packs more of a punch. If your kid could stand erect, it would be about the size of a fine cigar.

5

The Fifth Month

I found that the fifth month was about as good as a pregnancy month can get. The days of my wife's nausea and sore boobs were behind her, and it was another month or so before her heartburn and insomnia set in. My biggest frustration during the fifth month was that my wife's belly seemed to grow in direct proportion to the amount that my masculinity shrank. I was so busy running errands and doing housework that I could actually feel my testosterone level plummet. I bet you can relate. Your night out with the boys has been replaced by your night in with the laundry. Your racquetball calluses are softened by all that massage oil needed for nightly foot rubs. And your wife rejects you so often in bed that you feel as macho as Pee-wee Herman.

By now you may have even more hurdles to overcome. Maybe you'll have to endure your wife's constant crying jags as she watches commercials about deodorant and cat chow. Maybe you'll have some crying jags of your own when you're forced to spend the money you've been saving for new golf clubs on a closetful of maternity clothes. No matter what the reason, I'm sure that this month will give you some stumbling block to fall over.

But this fifth month is also one that will give your wife great pleasure. During this month your wife should be able to feel the baby kick for the first time.

So let's get to it, shall we? Let's see what obstacles lie just around the corner as we head into month number five.

What Goodies Await You This Month

Although some of your wife's first-trimester miseries are a thing of the past, several new ones have become a part of her present. Because of this, you'll have a new job description this month. In addition to being the maid, accountant, and caretaker, you're also going to be the household masseur. Yes, get your hands ready, because this month your wife will need to be rubbed. Between her backaches, sciatica, leg cramps, and sore feet, your palms will be greased more often than the maître d's at a four-star restaurant. I know it may be hard to constantly have to massage your wife's legs, feet, and backside, but take some comfort in knowing that the one ailment that can't be helped by massage are her hemorrhoids.

Her Symptoms and What You Can Do about Them

Your wife will be experiencing some side effects of pregnancy that you can help her tolerate. Here are a few:

Backache

- Massage her back either with or without a heated rub like BenGay.
- Put a heating pad on her back for no more than fifteen minutes at a time.
- If she feels she must lift anything, remind her to do it with her legs, not with her back. And move the sofa for her.

Sciatica

- Rub her butt, rub her butt, and rub her butt some more.
- Try not to laugh when she walks around all hunched over like an old lady.

Hemorrhoids

- Try to reduce constipation (see the list in Chapter 3, in the section called "Her Symptoms and What You Can Do about Them").
- Take a walk with her.
- Carry heavy items for her.
- Apply witch hazel pads to the affected area.
- Have her take tepid sitz baths.
- Remind her not to strain when she poops.

Leg Cramps

- Put a heating pad on her leg.
- Massage her leg with or without a heated rub like BenGay.
- Give your wife your pillow to elevate her legs at night.

My Wife Just Doesn't Understand Me

Although in some ways, pregnancy can bring a couple closer together, it can also push them further apart. The reason for this is that men tend to be afraid of their pregnant wives. And they have good reason to be. Their wives are big and bloated and can emit a gas so powerful that all of the houseplants have died. Because of this, husbands are reluctant to discuss certain things with their wives. They fear that if they do, it will be off with their heads, along with other important parts of their anatomies. So husbands tend to keep a few things to themselves.

One of these private thoughts is that fathers-to-be tend to feel ignored. This is especially true if you're used to being the dominant one in the relationship. For now, your place is in the background, while your wife takes center stage. Suddenly she's transformed into Gladys Knight and you are a mere Pip. Sure, you provide her with the support she needs in order to shine, but by doing so, you ignore your own needs. And so does everyone around you. Because of this you may feel abandoned.

It's also common for men to feel that their wives are too nervous about their health. They want them to lighten up and relax. They know that being pregnant is a worrisome time, but man, do they really have to worry so much? Their wives seem to fret about every little thing. Was their shower too hot? Did they stand too close to the microwave? Did they raise their hand too high and cause the umbilical cord to wrap around the baby's head? (No, that doesn't happen, but they've been listening to the old wives who tell them otherwise.) Women tend to read too many books and know far too well the possible dangers that can threaten their delicate little fetuses. They even make up a few perils of their own.

Another thing that you can't tell your wife is how difficult this pregnancy is for you—not that it is difficult for you in the same ways it is for her, but that you have some issues to deal with as well. You no longer come home after a hard day at work to a home-cooked meal. Your wife no longer asks you about your day, but goes on and on about her sore feet. Your relaxing night in front of the tube is interrupted by your wife's constant requests to watch her tummy to see if it moves.

Maybe you've felt some other frustrations but hesitate to tell them to your wife. You feel that she won't understand you—and you're probably right. I'm all for communication in a marriage and feel that it's a vital part of keeping it healthy. But there really are times, such as pregnancy (or when you forget to pay your wife's parking ticket and there's a warrant out for her arrest), that honest communication should be avoided at all costs. Instead, go vent to your guy pals who have been through this before. You'll feel better by getting this stuff out, and unlike your hormonal wife, they won't throw kitchen utensils at you.

Finding Out the Baby's Gender

There's nothing more exciting than the day you find out if you're having a boy or a girl. The only thing that may bring your spirits down is the fight that will ensue if you don't agree on which day that will be. These days couples have a choice of when to learn the gender of their offspring. They could find out during their ultrasound, through the genetic testing, or just by waiting until the delivery day.

Things were much simpler a few generations ago. Back then people didn't have a choice. There were no ultrasounds. No amnios. There was only a group of old wives who spun tales about how the gender is determined by how the woman carries or if her breasts are uneven. And when the earliest ultrasounds were developed, even they weren't always conclusive. Many an umbilical cord was confused with a penis, and a girl was born—instead of that well-endowed boy the parents were expecting.

But modern technology has changed all of that. These days, ultrasounds are fairly conclusive and are backed up with genetic testing. There are even ultrasound machines available that produce an image in almost perfect clarity. They're usually not covered by insurance, but you can rationalize the expense by thinking of it as your child's first professional portrait.

In our case, my wife wanted to know the sex as soon as possible, but I wanted to wait. I figured that there are so few genuine surprises in this world that I didn't want to deny myself one of the biggest ones of my lifetime. But because my wife was pregnant, and outweighed me by fifty pounds, I gave in. Truth be told, even though I knew that we were going to have a girl, I did receive a genuine surprise the day that she was delivered. That was when I found out how much the bill was going to be.

Even if both of you can agree when to find out the sex, you still may have to deal with something else. What if you're not happy with the baby's gender? I know that you've been going on about how all you really want is a healthy baby, but deep down you may really want a boy. Someone to pass on the family name. Someone to toss the pigskin around in the yard. Someone you can have too-high expectations for, and not show enough love to—just like your father did with you.

You wouldn't even know what to do with a girl anyway. You don't know proper tea party etiquette or how to French-braid hair. You don't know the intricacies of playing with Barbie dolls, and you think that Strawberry Shortcake is merely a dessert. And you don't have a clue as to how to change a girl's diaper because, to be honest, you've never quite understood the way their plumbing works. With boys it's one clean sweep. With girls, there are so many nooks and crannies to clean that every diaper change is like detailing a car.

Finding out the sex of your child is a big deal. But if you and your wife are arguing about when to find out, or if you're struggling with the letdown of the baby not being the gender that you had hoped for, I have one piece of advice: Get over it. When it comes to your baby's gender, it really is a win-win situation. Whether you find out now or later, whether it's a boy or a girl, you've still won the lottery and your grand prize will keep paying off for your entire lifetime.

How to Play the Pregnancy Game

Many men have a difficult time when their wives are pregnant. They're forever terrorized by their hormonal spouses, and each day passes at the speed of a chick flick. But if men can think of pregnancy as they do a sporting event, they'll have an easier time of winning the game.

The game of pregnancy is like any other sport you've played; it's all about earning more points than you give up by the time the game is over. Points are earned on a continual basis by doing compassionate and thoughtful things for your wife, and they're tallied on a daily basis.

But before you begin, just like any other good athlete, you'll need to train. You'll need muscles that you haven't used in years, maybe since so far back as when you were dating. Back in the courtship stage, you were in top condition. You texted your loved one every day just to say hello and brought her flowers for no reason. But that was years ago and by now your muscles have atrophied like a major leaguer before spring training.

So let's get down to the rules of the game.

Single-Point Plays
- Go with your wife to the obstetrician.
- Read a pregnancy book.
- Do the shopping because the smells bother her.
- Give your wife your pillow to sleep with to support her back.
- Tell your wife to go lie down and that you'll do the dishes tonight.
- DVR your wife's favorite show for her to watch after she's thrown up.
- Bring home all the takeout menus in the neighborhood so she doesn't have to cook.
- Keep watch at the men's bathroom so she can pee in private when the women's room is too crowded.

Two-Point Plays
- Buy your wife panty shields—she needs them and she knows that you hate to buy them.
- Carry your wife's heavy purse for her—you're being considerate and you're willing to look like a sissy.
- Go with your wife to buy maternity clothes, and tell her you think she looks wonderful in them. Not only

are you going shopping, but you're also being considerate, if not completely honest.

Unfortunately, just as quickly as points are earned, they can also be taken away. Out of nowhere, you can commit a technical foul that will strip you of your hard-earned points. If this happens, remain calm, come up with a new game plan, and get back in the game.

Fouls
- Tell her that you're too busy watching TV to help her carry in the groceries.
- Berate your spouse for not wearing her wedding ring when her fingers are too bloated.
- Disturb your wife while she's napping because you can't find the remote.
- Tell your wife that her roots are looking kind of dark.
- Tell your wife that her feet smell when you're rubbing them (actually, this is only a half point off, because at least you're rubbing them).

At the end of the nine-month game, tally up your points and see how you did. If you're ahead, you can use these extra points for the next game, which starts after your kid is born. But unlike this version, the next one lasts until your child goes away to college. In the next game, points are earned by changing more diapers, giving more baths, and doing more midnight feedings than your wife. But until the next event starts, don't forget to stretch and put on your protective cup.

What to Expect When She's Expanding

Some men have a problem with their wives' weight while they're pregnant. On some level, they expect them to gain weight during these nine months, but they're surprised by just how much weight it turns out to be. Little did they know that their svelte bride could one day weigh as much as the entire bridal party.

The amount of weight a pregnant woman packs on can vary dramatically. Some look like they have a little potbelly, while others look like they swallowed a potbellied pig. This difference takes place again after their kidlet is born, because women tend to lose weight at a different pace, too. Some snap right back into shape, while others snap back with the strength of the elastic in your old boxer shorts.

For some men, watching their wives with their newly voracious appetites causes problems. They know that their wife is eating for two, but does it have to be two linebackers? Every month you watch your wife's belly increase like a heated container of Jiffy Pop. But her baby weight doesn't stop there. It spreads all over her, until her arms are thick and her legs are bloated. And her cheeks look like she's storing food for a long, hard winter.

Don't feel bad if you have a hard time watching your wife eat more than she did before. It's hard to watch your wife's shape transform from that of an hourglass to that of a snow globe. Most men have a real issue with this, although they'd never say a word, especially to their wives. I know I had a problem with it myself.

My wife had a great figure before she conceived, but it didn't take long for her to lose it. In fact, she lost it so well that years later, she still doesn't know where it is. She's looked everywhere. She managed to find her old high school yearbook and a dozen socks she lost in the dryer, but her figure is still missing in action. The problem was that she got too big, too fast. She was in maternity clothes at three months, and even her doctor was concerned. He asked her if she had a history of giants in her family. But even that didn't stop her from eating like Ms. Pac-Man.

The truth is that your wife does have to pack on some pounds during pregnancy. On average, a pregnant woman should gain between twenty-five and thirty-five pounds in order to have a healthy baby. Anything less could jeopardize the baby's health. My wife gained so much that she could have given birth to several healthy kids.

You may be wondering why a woman has to gain up to thirty-five pounds when the kid tips the scale at maybe eight or nine pounds tops. It seems that even though the kid doesn't weigh much, the additional packing material needed to carry the kid does. Let me break down some of the additional cargo weight that your wife has to tote around:

- **Baby:** 7 pounds
- **Placenta:** 1 pound
- **Amniotic fluid:** 2 pounds
- **Added weight to the uterus:** 2 pounds
- **Extra blood volume:** 4 pounds
- **Bigger boob tissue:** 2 pounds
- **Various other retained fluids:** 4 pounds
- **Extra fat that Mother Nature wants to store to ensure that she'll have the additional calories needed in case her food supply is taken away:** 7 pounds

But even if your wife gains more than expected, don't worry. There's no definite correlation between how much weight she gains now and how heavy she'll be after the baby is born. I've seen some women who barely looked pregnant keep on more weight after delivery than one who gained seventy pounds. The good news is that "The Baby Delivery Diet" is an excellent weight-loss program, better than the Atkins and Scarsdale combined. On this diet, your wife should lose more than ten pounds in a matter of minutes. By the end of two weeks after delivery, she may drop about twenty pounds of excess weight. The only diet that could rival it would be "The Amputation Diet."

The Name Game

Unless you're one of the fortunate couples who already had their child's name picked out since before they got pregnant, you can expect this issue to be a rather hot topic. The problem with deciding on a name is that there are too many names to choose from. Names would be a lot easier to pick if they were regulated by the government or based on some common ground. For instance, when a writer needs a pen name, he might take his middle name and the street he lives on. Maybe when choosing a name for your kid you can use a similar kind of principle. Say, like the liquor that was consumed the night that your kid was conceived: "You remember my two boys, Tom Collins and Jack Daniels, and our little girl, Sex On The Beach."

When it comes to picking a name for your child, you have several ways to go. There are the usual categories to choose from, like trendy names, family names, biblical names, or old-fashioned names. Or you can be creative and make up a name that's hard to pronounce and that your kid won't even be able to spell until he's in sixth grade, or later if he goes to public school.

Each category has its own set of unique problems. Trendy names are so common that your kid could suffer whiplash from turning around to answer so often. Naming your child after a family member is thoughtful but can get tricky. In our case, religion got in the way. My wife is Jewish and can't name a child after a family member who's alive. I'm not Jewish, and in my family, firstborn sons are named after their fathers—in my case, Bob. But I wasn't so hip on naming a child after myself. First of all, I'm not a king, and second, it was always confusing when I was growing up to decipher which "Bob" was needed for a phone call, mail delivery, or to open a Christmas gift.

You may have another kind of problem. What if you love a family member, but aren't too wild about his or her name? In this case, many people just use the first letter of the person's name. I'm not such a fan of that method. What you're really saying is, "I love you but your name really sucks."

If you follow only one rule about how to pick your child's name, follow this one: Choose a name that gives your kid the least chance of getting picked on at school. If there was someone in class whose name or monogram was ripe for teasing, it was always teasing season. And that goes for your child's initials as well. R.A.T. or P.O.O. will always warrant an embarrassing laugh.

If you and your wife are having a difficult time thinking of a name, maybe I can help with the following ideas:

- **If you're going to find out the sex of your child before it's born, wait until after that to start picking names.** This way you'll cut out 50 percent of the options and 50 percent of the fighting necessary to agree upon a name.

- **Choose a middle name first.** There's a lot less pressure with the middle name because no matter what you choose, your kid is going to hate it anyway.

- **If you're both businesspeople, you may feel more comfortable agreeing upon the name using the same strategy that you would when forming any other merger.** Every month, each of you makes a list of your ten favorite names and numbers them one through ten (with ten being best). Then each of you chooses your favorite name from each other's list. Do this every month, and at the end of the nine months tally up the points. Then pick the top three and have your wife make the final decision. Sure, she may choose a name that may not be your number-one favorite, but on the flip side, she'll choose a name that you don't hate either. If you think it's unfair that she gets to make the final selection, just watch her in the throes of labor and you'll agree that this method is quite fair.

- **Even if you haven't decided on a name when you're in the delivery room, don't worry.** Many couples wait until after their child is born to choose its name. They want to see their kid first and pick a name that suits him. Luckily we didn't use that strategy or our daughter would be named "Slimy."

Looking back, I can't believe all the trouble and stress we had picking out a name for our daughter. The truth is that after all our effort, we rarely even call her by name. She's always "cupcake" or "Tinkerbell" or any number of sickeningly sweet nicknames. The only time we ever say her real name is when she's in trouble.

Heads, She Wins; Tails, You Lose

Even before she conceived, your wife and you may have had a friendly competition as to who was the most tired at the end of the day, or who was the most famished before dinner. But now that she's pregnant, the feud is not that friendly anymore and it's not much fun either, because you don't have a chance in hell of winning. Now that your wife has conceived, all bets are off—when a woman is pregnant, she trumps you every time.

By now you've learned to keep your mouth shut. You can't mention that you have a headache without her rambling on about her migraine. If you're hungry, she's famished. If you have to pee, she has to pee like a racehorse. You can't even burp in her presence without her complaining that her heartburn is so intense that she can iron her shirts from the inside.

What makes matters even more frustrating is that your wife wants you to share your feelings. In an attempt to feel an intimacy that you no longer share in your bedroom, she wants to connect with you on an emotional level (yeah, like that even remotely comes close). You can expect your conversation to go something like this:

You and your wife are sitting together on the sofa watching TV. During a commercial break she looks over at you.

HER: How are you doing, hon?

YOU: I'm fine, thanks.

HER: No, really. Tell me what's going on. Is something on your mind?

YOU (reluctantly): It's nothing, really, I'm just a little tired.

Suddenly she freezes and stares at you with contempt. She takes a deep breath and:

HER: You're tired! What do you have to be tired about? I'm the one who's tired. I have to lug myself around all day and can't get any sleep at night because I have to get up every ten seconds to pee. You try putting yourself back to sleep every ten seconds; it's no easy task let me tell you . . .

Her voice fades in the distance as you slump into the couch.

Sure, you could retaliate. God knows that you have plenty of ammunition. You could tell her that you're not getting much sleep either. Between her snoring, the grunts and groans she makes every time she gets up to pee, and the fact that you don't have a pillow because you gave it to her, you're lucky if you get any sleep at all. But you don't say anything. Instead you make a silent promise to yourself never to utter another word of complaint, because no matter what you have to say, she can say it louder.

There's really not any way to stop the pattern. It's been going on for countless generations before you, which explains why your forefathers had such a blank stare in the old family portraits. Just keep your mouth shut and know that during this process, your side of the sofa will get broken in that much faster.

How to Make a Will

Anyone who has taken Basic Responsibility 101 will tell you that a couple with a child must have a will. You probably never thought twice about it when you got married. From your strong grasp of the legal system (achieved from years of watching *Law & Order*) you knew that if you died, your wife would be entitled to everything you had anyway. But now that you're going to have a child, you have a valuable commodity to protect.

A will is crucial because without one, if you both die, your child may not be raised by someone you would have chosen. In fact, it may even be raised by a complete stranger. Instead of growing up with a close friend or relative, your sweet angel may fall into the clutches of social services. If you don't have your wishes in writing, you will be doing your child a great disservice.

The most difficult thing about writing a will is deciding upon a guardian for your child. Most of your relatives are fine in a once-a-year-family-reunion kind of way, but it's hard to imagine any of them raising your child on a full-time basis. Admitting this to each other may be difficult. Your wife may be upset that you don't want your child raised by her sister in the support group. And you may get hurt that she doesn't think your brother is worthy simply because he likes to make clothing for his cat.

If you thought that choosing a guardian was hard, wait until your next task: choosing a backup. The reason for the backup is in case your first choice is unable or unwilling to do it at the time of your death. If you had a tough time picking a first choice, choosing the runner-up may seem impossible. The pickings will be so slim that the cat thing won't sound that bad after all.

Once you choose a guardian, you must then pick the rest of your Death Cabinet members. You're going to need someone to execute the will. That person has to be responsible, able to handle a great deal of paperwork, and not care about you so much that he'll cry all over it. Next comes someone to handle your child's money until he or she is eighteen. Without it, your child may be denied basic necessities like food, shelter, and those trendy basketball shoes that all the other kids are wearing. The most obvious person to pick for this job is the guardian, but if that person is having financial problems or has always dreamed of owning a Ferrari, you may want to choose someone else.

Now it's time to start divvying up your things. If you don't list every asset that you have, it may cause a family ruckus. Your brothers and sisters, nieces and nephews, and aunts and uncles will all fight over your prized collection of *This Old House* magazines. Finally, you'll need to state in your will some of your basic requests, like what type of education you'd like Junior to have, along with important child-rearing advice, like whether or not you allow soda before bedtime.

There are several ways to make up a will. You could buy a software program and make one on your computer. You could traipse down to your local bookstore and buy a book that can show you how. The drawback to this approach is if you do it wrong, you won't be around to fix it. Even though hiring a lawyer is the most expensive way to go, it doesn't have to break the bank—and protecting your baby is worth it.

They Grow Up So Fast . . . Especially in Utero

As usual your baby has gone through some major changes this month, especially if you're having a girl. By the end of this month, your daughter's uterus will be formed and her vagina will start to develop. Now is the time that you can officially start keeping the boys away. Your child now has the capacity to hiccup. This happens quite often to fetuses. There must be a martini bar somewhere up in the fallopian tubes. By now your wife can easily feel your baby moving around. Although this was an incredible experience at the beginning, the baby has a habit of kicking in the middle of the night, so this miracle may already be wearing thin. By the end of this month your child weighs as much as a big bowl of chili fries (about a pound).

6

The Sixth Month

As I already discussed, one of the most frustrating aspects of pregnancy for men is that they're not allowed to complain about it. Even a passing comment about how tired we are of giving our wife all of those back rubs will get us more stares than Megan Fox in a string bikini. We'd be perceived as selfish, ungrateful, and completely undeserving of the blessing that's growing in our wife's belly. The reason for the harsh judgment is that no one truly understands what it's like to live with a pregnant woman. No one, of course, but another guy who is living with one, too.

Most people would grant that you have a few reasons to sulk. They'll concede that you'll have less sex and more chores than ever before, and that you have to live with a wife who gets cranky from time to time. But what they don't understand is how these aspects of living with a pregnant woman permeate every part of your life. How can you concentrate at work when your wife bombards you with a list of errands and complaints? How can you enjoy reading the sports page when your wife asks you to count the new crop of moles growing on her back? And how can you enjoy a good meal with your wife when she sucks all the food off your plate like a Shop-Vac? Sure, living with a pregnant woman won't kill you, but it can take the fun out of living.

But I'm here to tell you to keep a stiff upper lip (it may be the only part of you that can benefit from being stiff, anyway). Realize that at this point, the pregnancy is more than half over. You're past the fifty-yard line and well on your way to the end zone. At this late stage of the game, your baby's developed his organs, your wife's developed her hemorrhoids, and you've developed your patience.

This sixth month of pregnancy should reward you with a great payoff. Sometime during this month, you should finally be able to feel your baby kick! No longer will your wife tell you that it's kicking only to have you rush over, put your hand on her belly, and feel nothing but disappointment. Finally you can feel the steady, delicate thump of the life force inside that not only will make this pregnancy thing seem real to you, but will also give you a thrill strong enough to keep you going until the end of the game.

In between those miraculous thumps, why don't you take a moment and read about some of the new adventures that are in store for you this month. This way you can either face them head-on, or run fast in the opposite direction.

What Goodies Await You This Month

This should be a good month. It's not that your wife won't have any new pregnancy phenomena, it's just that these ailments won't be as troublesome as what went down the first trimester, or what await you in the next (just you wait!!). By this last month in the second trimester, your wife has settled into her pregnancy like a seasoned veteran. She's used to some sleepless nights and her mysterious aches and pains. So when this month's goodies set in, if they set in at all, they won't be as traumatic as the ones in the first trimester, when your wife was still a pregnancy rookie.

When my wife was expecting, she got almost every ailment in the book. Every negative aspect in her life was explained by the fact that she was reproducing. She had dry skin? It must be a side effect of pregnancy. Got a sharp pain in her side? Still another pregnancy ailment. Put my golf clubs in the driveway and ran over them three times? Yup, just her pregnancy at work yet again. It seemed that being pregnant was like one big "get out of jail free" card.

Her Symptoms and What You Can Do about Them

If your wife is blaming every unexplained bodily reaction on your child, just humor her. If she's blaming any of the following symptoms on her pregnancy, then you know that she is indeed telling the truth and you should comfort her as only you know how (or as how I'm going to explain to you now).

Pains under Her Uterus

These are sharp, quick pains that she'll feel at the bottom of her belly. They're caused by the stretching of ligaments under her uterus. They'll become more frequent as her pregnancy progresses and the baby becomes heavier to carry. These pains should go away as quickly as they come. You can sign her up for prenatal yoga or take her to the driving range to hit a bucket of balls. There's something about making the swing that some women find helpful.

Absentmindedness

- Have her write down all the things that she has to take care of.
- If she carries a cell phone, make sure that you keep the batteries charged for her.
- If she has anything really important that has to get done, do it for her.
- If you have anything you've ever wanted to confess, say it now. Chances are, she'll never remember it later on.

Pain and Numbness in Her Hands

- Have your wife ask her doctor if she has carpal tunnel syndrome.
- Get a splint from the pharmacy. It may give her some relief.
- Ask her doctor if she can take vitamin B6.

Tingling of Her Hands

No one knows for sure why this happens but they all agree that it isn't anything serious. The best remedy for this is to have your wife shake out her hands or move them around.

Itchy Tummy

- Rub her belly with moisturizing lotion.
- Draw her a warm bath and add a scoop of oatmeal flakes that you've put into a pair of her pantyhose (ask first!). If you don't have oatmeal, add two cups of milk or one cup of powdered milk.

The Secret to Making Your Wife Happy

I'm going to let you in on a little secret when it comes to handling women, especially pregnant ones. They want to put their husbands up on a pedestal. They want a strong man that they can look up to. A woman will worship her man up on a pedestal for keeping her safe and protected. She can feel his love shower over her as she hands him his cold beer. Trust me, fellas, as long as you're up there, you're in for less nagging and more nookie.

But if you ever stumble off your pedestal, there will be hell to pay. Some of the ways to fall off are apparent, like if you forget your anniversary or wink at a Hooters waitress. But other ways aren't quite as clear. So let me take a moment to clear some things up.

One way to fall off your pedestal is to act childish. Before your wife conceived, she may have fallen for your boyish charm, but those days are long gone. If you spend all day being a couch potato instead of bringing home the bacon, you're sure to take a fall from your throne. Your wife already has one baby in her tummy and doesn't need another one on the sofa. Now, more than ever, she needs you to step up to the plate and act like a man.

Another way to get into trouble is to act irresponsibly. This includes dropping a chunk of change on the latest smart phone when you can't afford to pay the regular phone bill. Now, if you get a speeding ticket, your wife won't get turned on thinking that she married a "bad boy." All that she'll focus on is the fact that you drove too fast and put your life in danger. How can you be so selfish to take the risk that your child might grow up without a father—and her without your weekly paycheck?

You're also guaranteed to slip off your tower if you put your own needs ahead of those of your family. Even though your baby isn't born yet, it still counts as part of the family. If you choose to play racquetball rather than go with your wife to an OB appointment, she'll see it as putting your family second. If you tell her that you don't want to go with her to register for baby gifts, all she'll hear is that you don't care. I know that you don't see it that way, but she will. For what it's worth, all of these "family" activities really are important, because they're creating a sense of unity.

If you're having a difficult time changing your lifestyle and behavior for a baby that doesn't even have skin yet, you need a change of attitude. You need to understand that the responsibility you have to your family begins as soon as the pregnancy stick turns blue. You may as well get practice giving up things and activities you enjoy now, because once your baby takes his first breath, it'll happen on an hourly basis. Either that, or hop into your Way Back machine, travel back in time to the night your kid was conceived, and get a good mental image of your mother.

What You Need to Know about Life Insurance

Before my wife got pregnant, I never gave a rat's ass about life insurance. Sure, it would have been nice to take out a huge policy for my wife just in case I croaked, but I thought it would give her too much incentive to kill me when I stayed out late with the guys. But now that we had a child on the way, my wife pushed me to get some.

When you first look into life insurance, you may find the process rather daunting. There are so many different types of policies to choose from, and so many boring agents to deal with, that you may be tempted to pass on it altogether. But don't. The reason that life insurance is so important when you're having a baby is pretty obvious. It's so that if you pass away, your family will be able to live in a comfortable manner while you rot away in the grave.

When deciding how large a policy you'll need to take out, there's a general rule of thumb. You'll need coverage for about ten times your average yearly salary. In some instances you may not need that much coverage. Your wife may bring home a good salary of her own. You may have other investments or assets that your family can use. Maybe your parents have agreed to put your child through college. Or maybe you're just a tightwad and can't rationalize such a high premium payment.

When picking an insurance policy, you will have a few different kinds to choose from. The most popular, and usually the most affordable, is term life. It's called "term" because the policy is only good for a certain amount of years. After that, you'll have to renew it at a sometimes higher rate. Term life is best for young, middle-income families with children. Usually the rates are quite low (a premium for $250,000 in coverage is about $150 to $200 per year) but will increase significantly if you're a smoker or have other health issues.

Another type of coverage is whole life. Simply put, this is a life insurance policy combined with an investment account. The premiums are higher but part of your check goes toward some kind of tax-deferred investment account. One good thing about these policies is that your rate is fixed forever. And if you ever need money, you can get cash back from it for important things like your kid's braces, or football season tickets.

It doesn't matter if you get term or whole life, a low premium or a high one—just get it. It's a wise thing to do to protect your loved ones, and can even make your life easier while you're still alive. It will take one big worry off your shoulders and one nagging wife off of your back.

How Much Does It Cost to Raise a Baby?

At some point in the pregnancy, I'm sure that your wife has told you that she doesn't feel like her body is hers anymore. In a way, you'll know how she feels, because you don't feel like your money is yours anymore either. You're shelling out for a kid who isn't even born yet! And you know it's going to get worse once Junior makes his actual appearance. With the high cost of video games, designer sneakers, bail money, and rehab, the cost of raising a child is skyrocketing. I wasn't prepared for the onslaught of expenses during the first year. I figured that between my wife's breastfeeding and the tiny amount of fabric needed to make baby clothes, the costs would be minimal. Was I ever wrong.

First-Year Expenses
Here are some of the additional expenses that I wasn't prepared for:

1. **Formula:** My daughter decided she was done with breast milk at six months and wanted to move on to the hard stuff. Not only did I have to spring for daily formula, but also the bottles, bottle sanitizers, and bottle warmers that go with it.

2. **Diapers:** Man, a kid can poop. And poop. And poop. And poop.

3. **Layette:** It's a fancy word for a baby's wardrobe. Because an infant has the potential for so many bodily functions to go awry, it needs as many wardrobe changes as Cher does during a concert. Plus, because the kid grows so fast, it'll need a whole new wardrobe every three months that first year.

4. **Postpartum clothing:** Your wife will need interim clothing for when she's too big for her pre-pregnancy clothes and too small for her maternity ones.

5. **Pediatrician bills:** I was shocked by how many checkups a baby needed during its first year. Babies have more examinations than the worst hypochondriac.

6. **Accessory playthings:** These include things like a swing, a wall bouncy, and a saucer.

7. **A video camera:** Of course, my irrational wife wanted the best to prove how much she loved the baby. And like all technology, by the following year, it had become outdated.

8. **A babysitter:** After a few months we decided to have a weekly date night. Sure, it managed to keep the romance alive, but it also managed to kill our budget.

9. **Cord blood:** There is another expense that may rear its costly little head. It's called cord blood storage. It is now possible to extract your baby's umbilical cord blood and store it for future use. It seems that your baby's umbilical cord contains blood called stem cells. These stem cells are used in new treatments for about forty life-threatening diseases. What was once tossed in hospital trash cans can now actually save lives. After

your child is delivered, the medical team can prepare the cord to be frozen, and you pay a monthly storage fee equivalent to that of basic cable. Then you wait until your child comes down with bone marrow failure, leukemia, or any number of blood disorders. If he or she does, then you'll be prepared. The cord blood will be a perfect match and it will give your child an excellent chance of survival. But, if your child doesn't become ill, you've wasted a hell of a lot of money and may secretly feel a bit cheated.

There are plenty of other expenses you may encounter during that first year, depending on your personal situation. You may want to pop for Mommy & Me classes, a nanny, a dermatologist to remove any of your wife's postpartum spider and varicose veins, a plastic surgeon to lift her breasts, and a marriage counselor to keep your marriage intact.

Although the list of expenses may be long, don't have an aneurysm just yet, especially if you haven't had a chance to set up your life insurance.

Saving a Few Bucks

If money is an issue, there are many things you can do to hold on to more of your income. If you're looking for ways to save a few bucks, consider some of the following ideas:

1. **When you pay for something in cash, put the change away at the end of the day.** It's shocking how much change you can save in a month.
2. **Start a regular savings plan.** Set up an account and pay yourself every month along with your bills.

3. **Use coupons but actually put away the money that you've saved.** If you save fifty cents on Twinkies, put the fifty cents into your savings account. Go to markets that double your coupons and you'll be saving twice as fast.

4. **Buy nonperishable items like toilet paper, batteries, and paper towels in bulk.**

5. **If your wife wants to stay at home after the baby is born, it's true that you'll be losing more income, but you'll be saving on expenses.** You won't need to pay for child care, her daily work lunches, expensive office attire, and the necessary haircuts, manicures, and pedicures that go along with it. You'll also save on car expenses like gas and maintenance and maybe even insurance. Most insurance carriers allow discounts for stay-at-home moms.

6. **Pay off your credit card debt.** Because of their high interest rates, this is your best way to save some dough. Either switch to a lower-interest card that doesn't charge an annual fee or combine all of your debt into one low-interest loan. You should also get rid of all but one credit card and pay in cash for everything except emergency expenses. And make sure that you pay your monthly bill on time to avoid late fees.

7. **If you finally are able to pay off your car, keep making the payments, but make them to yourself.**

8. **Take a brown-bag lunch to work.** This is a great way to save big money over time.

9. **Cut back on expenses.** Don't eat out. Skip that expensive cup of coffee from the coffee shop and take a thermos from home instead. Cancel magazine

subscriptions. Raise the deductible on your insurance policies. And if you find the inner strength to do so, reduce the number of cable channels that you subscribe to.

If you need more cost-saving tips, there are several good books to choose from. Head down to your local bookstore, or better yet, go to the library and check one out. Then you'll start saving right away.

Multiple Births

Because of the enormous increase in fertility treatments these days, more women will be pregnant with multiples than ever. Before these treatments were available, twins occurred in only about 1 out of every 100 births. Now their rate is about double that (even higher if you include Octomom!). The statistics have also risen for triplets, quadruplets, and so on. The reason for this increase is that conception hormones tend to increase the number of eggs that a woman releases every month. So, instead of having just one fertilized egg implant in the womb, there can be a whole litter of them.

Whenever there is more than one baby, there is usually more than one problem. It's very common for mothers of multiples to have exaggerated pregnancy symptoms like increased morning sickness, fatigue, and swelling. They can also have more severe backaches, heartburn, and overheating. Fathers of multiples are also affected. They tend to have more severe hair loss.

But although uncomfortable, none of these pregnancy ailments pose any serious risk to the babies, or your hairline. And even though women carrying multiples are automatically labeled as high-risk pregnancies, almost all of the babies are born healthy and happy and screaming as loud as the rest of them. So if you're the parent of multiples, relax. Chances are that the biggest dilemma you'll face is deciding where to set up all the extra cribs.

Even though the fate of your offspring is in the hands of a higher power, as well as the hands of ultrasound and lab technicians, there are some things you can do to ensure that your extra bundles of joy are extra healthy. First of all, it's even more important that your wife eats right. She'll need to consume more vitamins and nutrients than women carrying just one child. She'll also have to eat about 300 additional calories per kid, so you better stock up on pickles, ice cream, and just about everything else. Your wife will also need to gain more weight, about ten additional pounds per offspring. Also, if her birth plan consists of using a midwife, she'll have to go back to the drawing board. Women of multiples are urged to give birth in a hospital, where they're better prepared to handle medical emergencies. And finally, make sure that she goes to all of her doctor appointments—and there'll be more of them than if she were only carrying one child. Her doctor will have to monitor your wife and the babies more closely. It seems that multiple babies also make for multiple co-pays.

Twelve Things You Should Never Say to a Pregnant Woman

We men have a tendency to say some stupid things. We don't do it on purpose. There's no malice behind our ignorance. It's just that sometimes the filter that stops those things from leaking down from our brain and into our mouths allows some things to squeeze through. So let me do a service to all of mankind by tipping you off to some no-no's to avoid saying to your wife while she's pregnant:

1. "Hey, you have more nipple hair than I do."
2. "I never noticed the resemblance before, but you look a lot like the Pillsbury Doughboy."
3. "But I've seen other pregnant women work out at the gym."
4. "Can I get you a trough?"
5. "Good news, I started an office pool about whether you'll poop during delivery."
6. "You know, your butt really does look big in those jeans."
7. "Look, your feet are now bigger than mine!"
8. "Hey, you're blocking the TV . . . hell, you're blocking the whole wall."
9. "Can I use your maternity underwear to cover the barbecue?"
10. "I never knew stretch marks were so unattractive."
11. "If I connected all those new moles on your chest, it'd make a map of Texas."
12. "No."

This ends my public service announcement.

Oh, Her Achin' Back

One of the most abused parts of your wife's body is her back. When she's pregnant, it has to perform double duty by supporting both her and the offspring. As you can imagine, that's no easy feat. By the end of your wife's pregnancy, she'll be carrying around the additional weight of a small microwave and her spine will bow under the pressure.

Your wife's back is also being aggravated by the new pregnancy posture she's achieved to allow her to keep her balance. In order for her spine to make up for the weight of her protruding stomach, she's forced to arch her back and squeeze in her shoulder blades. Even though this causes strain on her back, it keeps her from falling flat on her face.

Like most pregnancy symptoms, her back pain will leave her as soon as the baby does. My wife was amazed by how great she felt the night that our daughter was born. For the first time in months, she slept in a bed instead of a chair. And she did so on her stomach. On top of that, she didn't have to feast on her usual dinner of a bucket o' Tums. I think she was more excited about being an ex-preggy than she was about being able to hold her baby. She'll never admit it, but I know her too well.

If your wife is suffering from a backache—and show me a pregnant woman who isn't—here are some things that you can do to help:

1. Draw her a warm bath.
2. Put a heating pad on her back (but for no more than fifteen minutes).
3. Rub her back with or without a heated rub like Ben-Gay.
4. Put slats under your bed to firm up the mattress. Soft mattresses tend to make her back even more sore.
5. Make sure that she sits in a hard, straight-back chair. Her back will feel better and you get the comfy leather club chair all to yourself.

6. Remind her to always make sure that she lifts with her legs, not with her back.
7. Carry her heavy purse or backpack for her.
8. Give her a full-body pregnancy pillow to sleep with. It will make her back feel better, but unfortunately for you, it'll take up most of the mattress.
9. Get her a pregnancy belt that lifts her stomach and supports her back. You can find these on the web and at baby stores.

I realize that having a pregnant wife can make you ache, too. You worry about your finances and you have to neglect your own needs in order to satisfy those of your wife. And although you feel like you're carrying the weight of the world on your shoulders, trust me, she's carrying an even bigger load. So be nice and help her take some of her pain away.

Playing the Pregnancy Card

If you play your cards right, not only will you be getting a baby out of this pregnancy, you'll also be getting other goodies as well. Being with a pregnant woman entitles you to many special privileges reserved for royalty, diplomats, and actors on the covers of tabloids. In fact, there are so many benefits to it that you just may think about keeping your wife barefoot and pregnant year-round.

The reason for this is simple: Even though to you, your wife is just someone who yells at you for not replacing the empty roll of toilet paper, to others she's a divine being because of the miracle growing within her belly. Others look at her as someone who's been touched by God. To them she's larger than life (yes, I know she really is larger than life, but you get my drift). Having a pregnant wife is like having a VIP pass to the world.

Some of the rewards that you'll reap when you're with her are:

1. **You'll get better parking spots.** You probably didn't notice it before, but many malls and crowded garages reserve prime parking spots for expectant women. They're usually located next to the handicapped parking. Also, if you are ever fighting someone over a parking spot and feel that you may lose the battle, have your wife get out and show him her belly. You'll usually win.

2. **You'll get seated faster at restaurants.** Many hostesses will seat a pregnant woman before anyone else. They know that it can be difficult standing for long periods of time. They know how hungry pregnant women can get. And, they know that if they're hungry, cranky isn't too far behind.

3. **You can decline a boring invitation without anyone getting hurt.** It used to be that you'd be dragged to a dull party or event. But now that your wife is pregnant, you'll have the perfect excuse to decline. Your wife can be tired, achy, nauseated, or any number of things that would prevent her from attending. Get used to it. Even after your wife delivers, the kid will give you years' worth of good excuses as well.

4. **You don't have to wait for her so long when she has to go to the bathroom at an event.** Usually there are long lines at women's restrooms. But now when they see your wife coming, the line of women will part like the Red Sea to let her through.

There is a downside to this upside, though. These special privileges are only granted when you're actually with your wife. Once she's gone, your magic powers will vanish. Your wife is the celebrity and you are but her mere assistant. So learn from him and ride her coattails for as long as you can.

Let Me Resent My Wife

We all know that being pregnant can create some disturbing physical conditions. But did you know that it can also create some disturbing psychological ones as well? And not just for your wife. You too will experience some symptoms of mental anguish over these nine long months, like jealousy, bitterness, and—my personal favorite—resentment.

There are many reasons to resent your wife when she's pregnant. She becomes the lead character in the show and you are a background extra. She demands attention, compassion, and a good chunk of your free time. Here are some other reasons why you may be feeling your resentment level rise.

Reasons That You Resent Your Wife

1. She gets to feel the miracle of the baby kicking, while you only get to feel your wife's kicks when you snore.
2. She gets to sleep on the mattress, and you're restricted to the edge of the bed.
3. She gets to eat whatever she wants, even if it's off your plate.

4. She gets a crapload of gifts.
5. She gets along with her mother.
6. She can recite every pregnancy fact, whether learned from her doctor or from a Popsicle stick.
7. She doesn't care about your problems.
8. She gets to be waited on whenever she wants.
9. She gets control of the thermostat.

But you're not the only one who's feeling bitter. Although you didn't think it possible for your wife to experience yet another mood, you should add resentment to the already endless list of emotions that she feels.

Reasons That Your Wife Resents You

1. You can eat, drink, breathe, or smoke anything that you want while she lives like a nun in a plastic bubble.
2. You can stay up and watch Jay Leno. She can't make it to *Glee*.
3. You can get out of a chair without grunting.
4. You can cough without wetting yourself.
5. You aren't so gassy that you need to cut one every minute. Well, maybe you are.
6. You don't have to drink milk.
7. You can't smell it when your neighbor takes a dump.
8. Your nipples don't leak.
9. You have the desire, stamina, and arm span to play with yourself whenever the urge hits you.

They Grow Up So Fast . . . Especially in Utero

During this month, the size of your kid's body is trying to catch up with its oversized head. Its ears are moving closer to their permanent position on each side of its head. If you're having a girl, she's quite busy finishing up her internal organs and making her eggs. Even at this tender age she's quite a good multitasker. You may be interested to know (or maybe a bit disgusted, too) that your child is coated in a thick white layer of a waxy substance called "vernix." It protects your baby from chapping, abrasions, and getting those really deep wrinkles in its fingers like you get after having soaked in a hot tub. By the end of this month your child will weigh about as much as a good-sized turkey leg (about two pounds).

7

The Seventh Month

Two trimesters down and one to go! Reaching the seventh month marks yet another hurdle in the track-and-field event of pregnancy. You've made it to the third and final trimester—the last lap of the race! You may think that nine months seems like an unbearably long time to reproduce. Most animals do it in far less time. Cats only take about two months. Mice do it in three weeks. In fact, if you were a tsetse fly, your wife would carry the fertilized egg for less than a day. Of course, she'd have to eat you a few days after copulation, but the tradeoff may be well worth it.

On one of the millions of baby shows my wife forced me to watch, I learned that human beings are actually born premature. Unlike most every other living creature, humans are one of the few that can't walk or speak or even feed themselves when they're born. They're totally helpless. Humans wouldn't really be physically ready to be born until they were one year old.

But there's one inherent flaw. A one-year-old baby would never be able to get out of the birth canal. Mother Nature has timed his birth perfectly to coincide with the size of his head and the size of your wife's pelvis. So, even if you're sick and tired of having a pregnant wife, keep in mind that if it weren't for the engineering skills of Mother Nature, you'd have to deal with it for an additional twelve months. So let's be nice to Mother Nature, and be sure to recycle.

Now that I've given your life a whole new perspective, let me take a moment to crush your renewed spirit like an old cigarette butt. Let me fill you in on more things to expect when your wife is expecting.

What Goodies Await You This Month

Get ready, get set, GO! Now that you're officially in the third trimester, it's time to get physical. But not the kind of physical that you had hoped for. From here on in, you'll be doing more hard labor than the guys on a chain gang. The reason for this is simple: By now, your wife's belly has grown so large she may not be able to bend over. That means that you'll be picking up things from the floor, tying her shoelaces, shaving her legs, and putting on her underwear (on her, not on you). Basically, anything that happens south of her border will be in your domain.

This last trimester also brings back an old friend of your wife's: fatigue. It may have gone away for a while during the second trimester, but it's back with a vengeance, and it's packed its big suitcase because it's here to stay.

Her Symptoms and What You Can Do about Them

As usual, there are a few more ailments to warn you about this month.

Heartburn

- Have her eat a lot of smaller meals rather than a few big ones.
- Have her avoid spicy or fried foods, or acidic ones like coffee and tomatoes.
- Give her an extra pillow so that she can sleep with her head elevated. Soon, she'll have to sleep in a chair.
- Buy her antacids that are approved by her doctor.
- Don't let her wear anything that's constricting around her waist (or where her waist used to be).

Overheating

With her metabolic rate much higher than usual, your wife will feel much warmer than normal. She'll sweat often and turn the air conditioner on no matter what the season.

- Get her some strong antiperspirant and keep your distance.
- Use her skin to cook yourself a grilled cheese sandwich.

Edema

Edema is the unfortunate condition of swollen ankles and feet caused by the fact that she's retaining more water than SpongeBob SquarePants.

- Her swelling tends to get worse in warm climates, so take her to the Swiss Alps or stick her in a meat locker.
- Hide her high-heeled shoes.
- Get her support hose.
- Make sure that she drinks at least eight 8-ounce glasses of water each day.

- If her hands and/or face become puffy, especially if it lasts more than a day, call her doctor.
- Encourage her to remove her rings if they feel tight.

Painful Kicking
- Don't take your wife to a rock concert or action movie. The vibrations make the kid kick more.
- Wait it out. By the thirty-second week, the baby will be so smushed that it won't be able to pack much of a punch.

How to Make Bed Rest More Tolerable

Having a wife on bed rest is like having a newborn in the house. You have to wait on her every need as she just lies there, helpless to do anything for herself. She'll nap throughout the day and scream at you for no reason. You may be jealous that your wife is living your lifelong dream of having to stay in bed all day and watch TV while people bring you things. But the truth of the matter is that bed rest isn't as great as it's cut out to be. It can be physically difficult for your wife to lie down all day. Her muscles will atrophy and she'll probably put on more weight than she should. It's also more boring than you would think. And I don't have to tell you that it will be difficult for you as well.

There are many reasons why your wife's doctor might put her on bed rest. She may be experiencing first-trimester bleeding, hypertension, or she may be at risk of preterm labor. The severity of her condition usually determines the severity of her bed rest. With less serious maladies, women are allowed enough time out of bed to fix a four-course meal, while others may not even have enough time on their feet to make a three-minute egg.

No matter how strict her bed rest limitations are, there will obviously be a lot more things for you to do. If you have other children in the house, it will be even more of a challenge because you'll have to take over most of their care as well.

I do have a few suggestions that can make your job a little easier:

1. **Get a pair of walkie-talkies so that you can stay in touch from any room of the house.** The downside is that even though doing this can save countless hikes up the stairs, it also makes it difficult to pretend that you can't hear her.

2. **Try to keep the basic staples by her bedside at all times.** She should have an ample supply of water, snacks, books, magazines, and videos handy. This will save you from making many little trips.

3. **If you have a laptop computer, set it up next to her.** She'll be amused for hours playing computer games and may even leave you alone for a while. If you don't have access to the Internet, get it. Then she can go online and do the family shopping so you don't have to. She can also chat with other women about bed rest on pregnancy websites.

4. **Beg her friends and family to come over and bring a casserole with them.**

5. **Get her a foam egg crate mattress to lie on to relieve her aches and pains.**

6. **Give her a project to tackle,** like getting boxes of photographs into an album, or learning a new language on audiotape.

7. **Put some alcohol wipes next to her bed.** If she can't take a shower, she can use these to feel refreshed and to take off the top layer of stink.

Sex in the Third Trimester

By the third trimester, sex can become a real effort. Not only is it hard to get your wife to agree to it, but because of her size and the laws of physics, it's a challenge just to get the parts to fit together. In addition, sometimes the man has problems with hopping into the sack. There are many reasons why your sex life may be in a coma. See if you can recognize your own:

1. **Some women are embarrassed by their new form.** They feel fat and don't want you to see them naked. They also have backaches and headaches and heartburn and don't have much desire for sex. Of course this may turn you on even more, since we guys get aroused when faced with a challenge.

2. **You hate to admit it, but you may be turned off by your pregnant wife's new physique.** Sure she has bigger boobs, but her nipples are big and scary. She's covered with skin problems, and sweats so much that she smells like a locker room. Also her vagina, if you're lucky enough to find it under that big belly, isn't as attractive as it used to be. It's dark and engorged and emits an unpleasant discharge. What was once a sweet-smelling rose has turned into one that's been newly fertilized.

3. **At this late stage, there's no denying that there's a kid inside there.** You don't want to create an additional soft spot or shoot anything in its eye during sex. You

also don't want your kid to fear for its life as it sees
this torpedo-like thing coming toward it again and
again. When it's born it may come out doing a rope-
a-dope trying to defend itself against you.

4. **You're afraid that if you have sex with your wife, you'll
break her bag of water and start labor too early.**

As you can see, this third trimester can be a tough one
when it comes to having sex. It's especially difficult for those
men who are completely turned on by their pregnant wives.
They love their Rubenesque curves, their glowing skin, and
their heaving bosoms. Their clothing is tighter. Their cleav-
age is deeper. And no matter what gross effects of pregnancy
they witness, these men are still rarin' to go.

In any case, you may be able to revive your sex life during the final weeks of pregnancy. If your wife has done her
research (and they all have), she knows that having intercourse is a good way to start labor. Just remember, when you
do have sex, savor every moment and retain those memories
like a camel retains water, because just like the camel, you
need to prepare yourself for the long drought ahead.

Ways You Can Help Your Klutzy Wife

Having a wife in her last trimester of pregnancy is like being
married to Mr. Magoo. She bumps into walls, she falls off
curbs, and she trips over every bump in the sidewalk. She's
like a one-woman comedy routine.

Why the new physical comedy act? To begin with, your
wife's joints are loosening up as her body readies for delivery.
Because of the hormone relaxin (yes, it's very aptly named),

her joints are extremely limber. She can contort her body into positions that only Gumby can achieve.

Second, because of some of her other pregnancy hormones, your wife's vision isn't as good as it was before she conceived. There's no need to buy expensive frames just yet; after she delivers, her eyesight will revert back to normal.

The third reason for your wife's clumsiness is obvious. She's getting so big that her center of gravity changes on almost an hourly basis. Her fingers are swollen, so it's hard for her to hold on to things, and her tummy's so large that she can't see hazards below her belly button, like a coffee table or ottoman.

My wife was about as clumsy as they came. She was forever bumping into things and knocking things over. But I learned some tricks that kept the comedy routine to a minimum:

1. **Carry your wife's purse.** It's hard enough for her to steer her ship without the additional weight on her barge. I know you'll feel unmanly toting around a girly handbag, but get used to it. Soon you'll be carrying around a diaper bag.

2. **Hide all of her high-heeled shoes if she's foolish enough to still be wearing them.** I don't see how women manage to walk in those things even when they're not pregnant.

3. **Whenever you walk together, hold her hand or put your arm around her waist area.** She'll think that you're being sweet, but what you're really doing is saving yourself the additional ultrasound bill after she falls down and thinks that she's lost the baby.

4. **Make sure that your wife's shoes fit properly.** My wife was warned about how much her feet were going to spread, so she bought bigger shoes before she even needed them. She flopped around in them like Bozo the Clown.

5. **Last, you should never let your wife inside stores that display expensive items.** If you do, there's a good chance you'll be the proud owner of a collection of broken porcelain figurines.

No matter how much you follow my simple guidelines, there is still a good chance that your wife will fall once or twice. I know that it's horrifying to witness your wife come crashing to the ground with enough force to register on the Richter scale, but relax. Your baby should be just fine. It's easy to think the worst, but the womb is like a bomb shelter. In most cases, it would take a blow as severe as a car crash to cause any damage to the baby. But if, after an incident, your wife leaks any amniotic fluid, or feels less fetal movement, take a trip to your doctor's office to check it out.

Paternity Leave

If your wife works, she's probably arranged to take off time from her job to stay at home with the newborn. Many working women are entitled to three months of maternity leave. But did you know that you may be entitled to take leave from work yourself?

Paternity leave isn't automatically offered by every employer. You should check your company's policy as soon as you know you're going to have a baby (or before). Under the Family and Medical Leave Act, most employees of larger companies (fifty employees or more) now have the legal right to up to twelve weeks of unpaid leave when they have a new baby. To be qualified, you have to have worked at a company for at least a year (or 1,250 hours). If it turns out that the company you work for offers paternity leave and you qualify, you have to give your employer a month's notice before you can take the time off.

The Family and Medical Leave Act applies to both men and women, but you're likely to find that the "unpaid" part of it almost always applies to men, while many employers will offer women at least partially paid leave. (In some cases, women have to be insured for short-term disability in order to obtain this benefit.) So, yes, your desk and all the stuff on it will still be there when you return from your leave of absence, but, no, you won't be getting your paycheck for doing such a fine job of staying home and changing all those diapers. Usually, you're not legally entitled to pay during paternity leave unless you live in California. California was the first state to guarantee dads paid leave for a few days up to a few weeks. It's almost enough to make you want to move there, or better yet, to Sweden, where new parents are allowed a total of 450 days of leave that can be taken by either the husband or the wife. And, if you lived in Stockholm, there's also a good chance that your wife would be a willowy blond Swedish woman and . . . um, what was I saying? Oh yeah, paternity leave.

If you do take advantage of paternity leave, your company is required to keep up your health benefits while you're gone. You'll have to discuss with them how health insurance payments will be made. With any situation that involves taking time off from your job or continuing your insurance, you should follow two simple rules:

1. Discuss it with your boss or human resources department as early as possible.
2. Once you find out what you're eligible for, get it in writing. Trust me, you don't even want to think about not having insurance to pay all the huge medical bills that a tiny baby can ring up in its first few months of life. Compared to those expenses, having to pay for college would be like buying your kid an ice cream cone with extra sprinkles.

Even if your employer doesn't offer paternity leave, you may find other ways to play hooky and be a house dad for a while. You could use vacation days or sick days that you've accumulated during your employment. Or you can work overtime and bank the hours now to stay at home later. Or if all else fails, you could talk to your boss about taking a leave of absence beyond what is legally required or normally offered by your company.

But don't have any misconceptions about paternity leave. It's no day in the park. Even though you're not at the office, you'll still be hard at work. You'll do laundry, run errands, and greet and feed visitors. And, of course, you'll have to do the endless odd jobs needed to keep the baby alive until the next day. Since your wife can barely walk after giving birth, you will be doing most of the grunt work. But don't despair, because paternity leave can be very educational. You will indeed learn a thing or two. You'll learn why taking care of a baby is the hardest job you'll ever have. You'll learn how to multitask in order to get all the jobs done. And you'll learn why Prozac is one of the most prescribed medications on the market today.

The Best Gifts to Buy Your Achy Breaky Wife

Although giving your wife the gift of a new life is nice, you should consider getting her some other things as well. May I suggest some pregnancy favorites to help make her pains less painful? Most of the following gift ideas can be purchased from baby stores, discount stores, catalogs, or over the Internet.

1. **An egg crate mattress.** If your wife is suffering from aches and pains, or on long-term bed rest, this is a great gift. It will provide her with the perfect place to relax her muscles.
2. **A pregnancy pillow.** It's a body-sized pillow that gives her great comfort through the night. It's a pregnant woman's version of a blowup doll. It supports her back, hips, and stomach and can make for a much more comfortable night's sleep.
3. **A foot massager.** It vibrates away the tension and pain in her feet. Not only will she love it, but you will too, because it will get you out of those daily foot massages.
4. **A cooling neck pillow.** Before using this kind of pillow, put it into the fridge to chill. When your wife puts it around her neck it'll cool her down like buttermilk dressing on a Buffalo wing.
5. **A shaver that doesn't need lather to work.** Because shaving her legs can be quite a workout, make it

easier for her by getting her one of those newfangled shavers—one brand is called Intuition—that work without shaving cream. You'll like it, too, because at some point, the chore of shaving your wife's legs will be added to your already overloaded list.

6. **A belt supporter.** This is a thick elastic band that fits under her belly and across her back. What it does is lift some of the weight off of her front and helps with any backaches she may have. If you have a bit of a potbelly yourself, get two. Maybe you can get some kind of a discount.

7. **A back massager.** If you're getting tired of giving your wife nightly rubdowns, invest in a back massager. They're sold in a variety of places, from Brookstone to Target, and they come in several different styles and prices.

8. **Massage lotion.** Back rubs are made infinitely better with the addition of massage oil. If you want to keep the rubs to a minimum length of time, my advice is to buy those that are scented with food flavors like vanilla or strawberry. This way she may get a craving, and her desire for food could overpower her desire for the massage.

9. **A giant-sized container of Tums.** If your budget is low and her heartburn is high, give her this gift, which she's sure to love.

Check maternity stores and catalogs occasionally. It seems that every month, someone has created a new product guaranteed to make a pregnant woman's life easier. The only thing I can think of that would be guaranteed to work would be a device that could carry the baby for her.

Babies "R" Expensive

Sometime during this month, it'll hit you that the baby will be here soon. And he'll need someplace to sleep. He also deserves a nice place to have his diapers changed and a thing or two to wear. When your wife asks you to come with her to the baby store to get some baby necessities, don't say, "I've made it this far without knowing the difference between an umbrella stroller and a Snap-N-Go, and I don't have much desire to learn now." Instead, tag along like a good little boy because if you don't, you'll need a new place to sleep as well.

The first time I went to one of these baby stores, I was dumbstruck. I had no idea how many essentials were needed to keep a baby comfortable. There were cribs and strollers and high chairs and playpens, bouncies and walkers, and swing sets and saucers. And each category had a subcategory of its own.

Take the stroller, for instance. There are jogger strollers, umbrella strollers, stroller frames that hold the infant car seat, and strollers for travel that fold up so small that you can almost stick it in your wallet. If you can ever decide on what kind of stroller you want, then you have to choose from the various accouterments that go along with it. There are stroller bar toys, stroller sun protectors, stroller cup attachments, and even a special stroller music system in case Junior wants to rock out on his way to Gymboree.

As you walk down the endless aisles you'll see your shrinking bank balance flash before your eyes. Many of these "necessities" can be pricey. And, to make matters worse, your wife's warped belief system pops up again. She thinks that if you love your baby, you'll buy it only the best. The bassinet sheets will have a higher thread count than your own. The

high chair will be crafted finer than Stickley furniture. And
the car seat she'll buy will have finer leather than your own
car seat . . . and you drive a Mercedes.

It's then that you realize your baby will be living a better
life than you are. You can try to talk some sense into your
wife. You can explain to her that Junior can't truly appreciate the 24-karat-gold trim on his baby book, since he can
only see in black and white, but trust me, she won't listen.

There really is no right way and wrong way to buy
things for your baby. Sure, some are more expensive, but
that doesn't always mean that they're better. I prefer the
simpler items myself. They're easier to assemble, easier to
use, and easier on your budget. You also don't need to buy
every kind of item that the store sells, even though they'll
try to convince her otherwise. The only "must have" item
that I recommend is one of those vibrating bouncy chairs.
It seems that vibrations pleasure your baby as much as they
do your wife. They sell all different kinds of bouncies, some
with toys, some that play music, but the vibrating kind is
the one that's preferred by four out of five dentists (assuming
that these dentists are new dads).

A frustrating part about most baby stuff is that it's
only good for a limited time frame. Most of the items that
babies use during their first year are only good for a couple
of months. For instance, my wife bought a Moses carrier. In
case you don't know (and why would you?), it's a padded
basket with carrying handles that's about the size of a loaf
of French bread. You can put your newborn inside of it and
carry it around the house with you from room to room. Yes,
it's a cute little basket, but a newborn grows so fast that it
can only fit in it for about an hour and a half. The solution
to this problem is to look for baby items that can convert to

other items. They're like baby Transformers. For instance, they make floor toys that convert into walkers, car seats that can be used as baby carriers, and high chairs that recline so that your kid can nap after exhausting itself by throwing food all over the room.

The most expensive place to go for baby goodies are the specialty boutique baby stores. There's something about those enchanting pastel-colored wonderlands that makes a woman's maternal instinct kick into high gear. They fantasize about nestling their newborns onto cashmere blankets and designer crib bumpers. My biggest cost-saving tip is to bypass the boutiques altogether and shop exclusively at discount stores, garage sales, and secondhand stores. Or better yet, borrow anything you can, except for an older crib (wide spaces between slats can trap your baby's head) or a car seat, unless it's fairly new and you're sure that it's never been in an accident. (Car seats are like condoms and are only good for one blowout.) Although this way of shopping sounds like a smart plan, it won't be easy to convince your wife to shop anywhere other than a specialty baby store.

By the time your next kid comes, things will be much easier and much less costly. Your wife will have satisfied her need for cashmere baby goods. With her second child, she'll just stick the kid in a sock drawer and dress it in puke-stained hand-me-downs. But for now, it's the crème de la crème for her little cream puff, unless you can convince her otherwise.

Get a Plan in Writing

Before you and your wife got married, the two of you had many things to work out. You had to figure out who would do the laundry, who was going to be the family cook, and who would scoop up the dog poop in the backyard. By now all of the domestic chores have been divvied up and the system is running smoothly.

But soon there'll be a seven-pound wrench in the works. Said wrench will throw your whole system out of whack. It will cause you to rethink your job assignments, as well as force you to add many others to the list.

It's common for marriages to go awry after the baby is born. Life as you knew it is over and you have to adjust yourselves to your new one. You'll both be suffering from enormous sleep deprivation and, if your wife chooses to breastfeed, you'll continue to live on a hormonal roller coaster. I know of numerous couples who have gone to marriage counselors during that first tumultuous year after delivery. So, in hopes of saving you time and money, and avoiding having to examine your relationship with your mother, here are a few things that you should decide upon now.

1. **Who will change the diapers?** How will the chore be divvied up? Will you alternate, or will one do it during the day while the other does it at night?

2. **Who will do the feedings?** Are you willing to get up throughout the night or do you expect your wife to do it all? Will one of you feed the kid while the other one puts it back to sleep? You may think that if she breastfeeds that she'll be in charge of it all, but there's an invention called a breast pump that will make you think again. When deciding, make sure that she's aware you'll have a more difficult time with nightly feedings than she would, since you have to heat the bottles and her breasts are self-warming.

3. **Who gets to sleep in?** Since it only takes one person to get up when the baby does, who will get up and who will sleep in? Are you the morning person in the family or is she? Will you alternate?

4. **Who will bathe the baby?** Bathing an infant can be a great activity. It's a fairly simple task, since your kid doesn't work up a sweat and has hardly any hair to wash. Most pediatricians recommend that you don't even use soap on newborns. And besides, usually the baby loves taking a bath and it makes precious noises. But, after doing it a hundred thousand times, the job can wear pretty thin. So, again, do you plan to alternate or do it like the dishes: one wash, one dry?

5. **Who cuts the nails?** Baby's nails grow fast and if they aren't cut often can scratch the baby's face. Since the nails are so tiny and the trimmers so large, I advise that this task go to the parent with the better vision.

6. **Who gets to clean out its bellybutton stub?** Granted, this chore only needs to be done for a couple of weeks, but it isn't for the weak of heart.

7. **Who will go to the pediatrician?** Infants need checkups often during the first year. Plus there may be many visits in between due to even simple problems, like a cold. Will you alternate, or will the task go to whomever works closest to home?

These are but a few of the issues that couples can fight about during the first few months. I'm not saying that you have to write anything down in stone right now. Things will certainly change once the baby arrives. This list is merely for discussion to see if you're on the same page about your parental responsibilities. And, if you discover that your expectations are different, arguing about it now will be a whole lot easier, while it's still the calm before the storm.

Keep in mind that there is plenty of room to negotiate. If you can't stomach the thought of changing poopy diapers, maybe you can swap for more bathing duty. If you need more sleep at night before you have to go to work, tell her she can sleep in on the weekends. Like anything else in life, it's all a matter of negotiation.

They Grow Up So Fast ... Especially in Utero

During this seventh month your child is getting used to hearing family voices, so now is the time to stop all that cussing and swearing. The big news is that if you're having a boy, this is the time when he'll actually get his balls. He also is becoming quite hairy. His eyebrows are forming and he even has a hairier chest and back than you do. The truth is that his whole body is now covered with fine downy hair called "lanugo." Your baby's hands have started to grasp onto things, so he can start playing with himself if he so desires. By the end of this month your baby weighs in at close to sixteen Quarter Pounders (that's four pounds, if you're too sleep-deprived to figure it out).

8

The Eighth Month

By the eighth month, you're missing your wife with a vengeance. It's not that she went anywhere. In fact, you can't seem to get rid of her no matter how hard you try. But the woman next to you in no way resembles the one that you married.

Having a pregnant wife is like dating a famous actress. They're both insecure about their looks. They both need constant attention. And they both think that they're fat. They're also temperamental, need new clothing every month, and, everywhere they go, people stare and want to touch them.

In other ways, it can be more like living with your mom when you were a teenager. She orders you around all the time. She yells if you don't do your chores. She insists that you stop smoking and forbids you to get a motorcycle. She bans you from doing anything dangerous and from staying out late with your friends. She would like nothing better than if you stayed home every day to keep her company while she knits.

I sincerely hope that your wife's pregnancy doesn't cause her to suffer from multiple personalities. But if she does,

you might want to give your CPA a call. You may be entitled to more dependents than you're actually claiming. But
until then, let's push ahead into this eighth, and almost final,
month of pregnancy.

What Goodies Await You This Month

Let me warn you about something. Now that you're nearing
the homestretch, things are going to get tough. What morning sickness was to the beginning of pregnancy, heartburn is
to the end. If your wife is anything like mine, heartburn will
make your wife completely miserable. In the past, there were
only certain foods that my wife ate that caused her distress.
Now even swallowing her own saliva made her miserable.

   Your wife's heartburn is difficult for her to handle at
night. It seems that acid reflux is a problem for preggos
because when they lie down, their stomach acid rises up
into their esophagus. Therefore, they have to stay erect at all
times. You, on the other hand, may never be. The last thing
your wife will want to do is lie down and have sex. But even
though you may not get any action in the sack, you may
finally get some rest in it. Because of her heartburn, your
wife may prefer to sleep sitting up in a chair, which means
that you can have the bed all to yourself.

Her Symptoms and What You Can Do about Them

In addition to your wife's increased heartburn, here are some
other surprises that are in store for you. Johnny, let's tell
them what goodies they've won!

Braxton-Hicks

As she heads into her ninth month, her Braxton-Hicks contractions may feel stronger and last longer.

- Have her change positions or take a warm bath.
- Call the doctor if she has more than four of them an hour or if she has pains in her back, stomach, or pelvis. You should also call if she has unusual discharge, or should I say more unusual than the unusual one that she has now.

Incontinence

Your wife may pee when she laughs, sneezes, or coughs. Here's what to do:

- Have her do her Kegel exercises and buy her plenty of panty shields.
- Keep in mind that this might not be the best time for you to ask her for a lap dance.

How to Handle the Other Kids in Your House

I've never had to face the hurdle of how to deal with other children. We only have one daughter, and at this point, that's just about all we can handle. In fact, I'm not quite sure what makes a couple with one screaming, temperamental, up-all-night child say, "Hey, let's go through this madness again!"

But I do have a theory about it. I think that there are actually four different kinds of babies that are born. There are the obvious kinds like boys and girls, but there are two additional categories as well: easy and difficult. If you're lucky and have spent your life helping old ladies cross the street, you may be blessed with an easy kid: the kind that can sleep through the night just weeks after she's been brought home, the kind that only cries when hungry or wet, and the kind that can entertain herself for hours on end. These are the kinds of children that are destined to have siblings. Mine is the kind that's destined to have goldfish.

In some ways, living through another pregnancy while having a toddler in tow may be easier. Even though your wife is still sick, hormonal, and tired, she won't yell at you as much or slack off as often, because she has a small child to take care of. Also, she's been through all the pregnancy stuff before so she doesn't freak out if the baby doesn't meet its quota of hourly fetal movements. She doesn't have time to even count them. Also, you don't have to spend a fortune on baby stuff because you already have the basic staples, and, as mentioned in the previous chapter, by now your wife should be over her "I must buy everything at an expensive boutique" syndrome. And better still, you don't have to go to any more birthing classes.

Chances are that your firstborn will love that mommy is pregnant. She'll kiss her growing belly and is excited about the idea of having a baby brother or sister. She doesn't quite grasp the concept that soon, she'll get as much attention as the dog has since she's been born.

Most experts agree that there are guidelines to follow when a second baby makes four.

1. **Don't tell your firstborn that you're pregnant until you're at least three months along.**
2. **Read books to him or her about what life will be like once the baby is born.**

3. **Get your toddler a doll and play baby with her (or him).**
4. **Have your firstborn help pick out a name, sheets, and toys for the new baby.** If you want to give your newborn any of your toddler's old things, make sure that it's okay with the toddler first.
5. **When you come home from the hospital, you should carry the new baby into the house so that your wife can give attention to the firstborn.**
6. **If your wife is not supposed to lift anything heavy—such as the firstborn child—advise her to blame something other than the pregnancy.** Doing this will fend off the resentment process. Make up another reason—little kids are pretty gullible, you know.
7. **If you plan on using your child's crib for the baby,** have the older sibling move to a bed way before the baby is born so it's not like the baby is taking over his or her turf.

Just because things may be easier during the pregnancy stage, don't get your hopes up that they will be easier on the other end, too. From what I've heard, you may be in for some stressful times after the birth of your second child. It may take you longer to bond with your newborn because you don't get to spend as much time with it. Your wife may have even less of a sex drive than she did after the birth of her first (as if that's even possible). I've also heard that the first year after your second child can be the hardest year of your marriage. As I said, I'm no expert. Maybe having a second child could even make things easier. With another kid in the house, your wife is much less likely to be finding fault with you. You'll be lucky if she even notices that you're still there at all.

Bondage

Let's get one thing straight from the get-go. There is no way to bond with your unborn child with the same intensity that your wife does. And there's not one thing that you can do about it, no matter how hard you try or how much your wife wants you to. This fact may cause your wife to get upset. She wants you to feel the same closeness that she has, but what she doesn't understand is that she has an unfair advantage: the baby is literally attached to her. How can you compete with that? She can feel the baby moving around and kicking. She can feel the effects it has on her body on an hourly basis. You, on the other hand, walk around most of the day without even remembering the pregnancy.

But you shouldn't feel bad about this. Most men are as unaware as you are and don't feel a strong attachment toward the baby until it comes out. Right now, the baby is just a list of chores that you have to get done. Paint the baby's room. Clean out the kitty litter. Read those pregnancy books. Right now your baby is not completely real; it's just something that eats up all your free time.

There are but a few moments during your wife's pregnancy when you may experience the similar bonding intensity that your wife does, but these moments will be few and far between. Even so, it will hit you like a bolt of electricity, like the thrill you get when you see a falling star, or a game-winning three-pointer. These are those moments of pregnancy:

How Long the Excitement Lasts

The Moment	Length Your Excitement Lasts
When the pregnancy test comes back positive	Two days
When you hear the baby's heartbeat for the first time	Half a day
When you see the ultrasound	Three days
Every time you see the photo of the ultrasound	About thirty seconds a pop
Every time you feel the baby kick	About ten minutes per kick

So, during the entire nine-month gestation period, your baby seems real for about a week, week-and-a-half tops. How can you possibly be expected to bond with something that you don't even recognize as being there for more than 90 percent of the pregnancy? Even so, your wife is going to keep on pushing you. She'll show you articles that substantiate the fact that if you read to your baby in utero, it will become more familiar with your voice and therefore become calmer in your presence after it's born.

If your wife is really pressuring you to talk to her stomach and you feel uncomfortable making conversation with her belly button, I have some advice that may make the awkward experience easier. First of all, wait until your wife has completed her second trimester. Before that time your kid's ears don't really work yet, so it doesn't stand a chance of picking up your voice. Next, instead of struggling to think of something to say, read to it from a magazine. What does it matter, really? Your kid doesn't understand what you're saying anyway, and it might pick up your exuberance when reading *Sports Illustrated*. It may even look forward to the swimsuit edition as much as you do.

Goodbye, Peter Pan

Face it. All men are still kids at heart. Sure, we go to work dressed like grownups wearing pressed shirts and clean underwear (well, maybe we don't go that far), but deep down, all we want to do is play. Once we got married, we had to give up a part of our boyhood. We couldn't stay out after sundown. We couldn't play with the girl next door. But that was okay because there were some good parts about being married, like the home-cooked meals and having someone around to pick up our dirty socks from the floor. But now that you're expecting a baby, say adios to your inner Peter Pan.

There's no way to deny it any longer. Expecting a child is like hammering the last nail in the coffin of irresponsibility. From here on in your life is full of "no mores." No more sleeping in on Sundays. No more spending all your money on gadgets. And no more sitting around all weekend watching sports. Sure, you could still be a father and act in this juvenile manner, but you'll be doing it every other weekend and alternate holidays.

From here on in, your days will be spent changing diapers and safety-proofing the house. The only four-letter words you'll be allowed to use will be milk, burp, and poop. And you're going to have to suck up to your boss for job security for the next eighteen years. From now on, you need to care about your company's health plan and your credit card's interest rate.

No matter how much you fight it, you'll have to become a responsible man. The world will no longer revolve around you and your endless needs. But don't despair. There are a few benefits to growing up. After a lifetime of wondering, you may finally learn what the term "escrow" means.

I don't mean to sound like such a downer. There will still be brief moments when you can have fun and eat cake, but there won't be any more girls jumping out of them.

How to Help Your Wife Sleep So You Can Too

By the eighth month, your wife will have more trouble sleeping than ever before. During the first trimester she felt tired all the time as her body grew accustomed to growing a human being in her belly. But back then she had the luxury of sleeping whenever the mood hit her. Now all that has changed. For even though her fatigue is as big as ever, so is her size, making a good night's sleep impossible. She's also suffering from heartburn, backache, sciatica, and the baby's nightly Tae Kwon Do lessons. If she ever does find her way to the Land of Nod, her visit will be short because of her frequent need to pee. Some say that this sleeplessness is good practice for the sleep deprivation you'll experience after the baby comes. But I disagree. I don't think any amount of practice makes one used to that.

Here are some tricks to fill her nights with more Zs.

1. **If her doctor approves, go to the drugstore and get her an over-the-counter antihistamine.** Yes, I know that her problem with sleeping is caused by a stuffed belly, not a stuffed nose (although she probably has that, too), but an antihistamine has the added benefit of making one drowsy. By taking it, she just may feel tired enough to doze off.

2. **Put up nightlights to mark her way to the bathroom and in the bathroom itself.** My wife would complain that

after she got up to pee it was hard for her to fall back to sleep because switching on the bright bathroom light would shock her system.

3. **If her heartburn is getting bad, get her one of those pillows that looks like a big wedge of cheese.** This way her body can be at a 45-degree angle and keep her stomach acid in her stomach, where it belongs.

4. **If your wife is up half the night, you should subscribe to as many cable channels as you can afford to keep her entertained so she'll leave you alone.**

I hope that by using some of these methods, your wife can get a good night's sleep and wake up rested and refreshed. That way she'll have the energy she so desperately needs to yell at you throughout the next day.

If Men Had Babies

If you're anything like me, there's one phrase that you keep hearing over and over again during your wife's pregnancy. It's "If men had babies, there wouldn't be any kids." And again, if you're like me, you think that saying is a load of crap. Sure, if given a choice, most men would pass on carrying the child for nine months and having to go through a long and painful delivery. But that doesn't mean we couldn't handle it.

Don't get me wrong. I have no desire to take over the task. I admit that there were moments when I felt jealous my wife was the one who was pregnant. I wanted to experience the sensation of the baby kicking inside me. I wanted to be granted permission to eat for two (actually my wife ate for three or four, but who's counting). But not once have I ever looked at a pregnant woman and wanted to trade places with her. I've never had the desire to waddle or to order shoes in size triple E wide. And even though if I were pregnant, I could play with gigantic boobs anytime I felt like it, I still wouldn't trade in my testes for a couple of ovaries. I'm only saying that, if the situation were reversed, men could certainly handle the hardships of pregnancy as well, if not better, than women.

So the next time you hear the expression "If men had babies, there wouldn't be any kids," realize that the only reason this saying exists is to give women the false belief that they are superior to men. Of course, don't tell this to your wife, or she'll give you a good tongue-lashing and send you to your room.

Things to Do While You Still Can

Time is running out. As you've probably been warned, once your baby arrives you won't be able to do many of the fun activities that you now take for granted. That's why, with only a few weeks left to go, you should partake of as many of these activities as possible while you still can.

If you're old enough, you may remember the Schick Centers that exploded during the '80s to help smokers quit their habit. Schick's technique was to have smokers chain-smoke for long periods of time until they were so disgusted and nauseated, they didn't have the desire to smoke anymore. My advice is that you should use that same technique now.

For as long as you're able, you should exhaust yourself with fun and frolic until you're disgusted and nauseated, so that when your little bundle arrives, you never have the desire to do any of these fun things again. Even if this technique doesn't work, at least you will have had a last bit of fun before you become too old to remember how.

Your List of Possible Final Hurrahs

- Travel, travel, travel (remember, your wife can't fly after her seventh month).
- Play eighteen holes of golf all on the same day.
- Get together for a poker night.
- Go away for a romantic weekend getaway.
- Curse anytime you want.
- Watch an entire day of sports without feeling guilty.
- Have loud sex.
- Build something that requires concentration.
- Go to a double feature.
- Sleep late.
- Watch television with the volume turned up really loud.
- Eat an uninterrupted meal.

I don't mean to sound so negative. You'll still have plenty of stimulating activities to participate in even after the baby arrives. But they'll be stimulating in different ways, like trying to change your son's poopy diaper without getting peed on.

Brainless

One of the first things that attracted me to my wife was her level of intelligence. She had so many facts and figures stored in her head that it was like being married to a Trivial Pursuit game. She knew more useless information than anyone I'd ever met. She could recite the alphabet backward as fast as she could forward. She knew how many bones are in the human body, and the sign language for "dead turtle." She was always a big hit at cocktail parties. But once my wife was pregnant, I realized that my kid was not only depleting her of her vitamins and nutrients, it was sucking her dry of brain cells, too.

It seemed that as our kid was growing bigger, my wife was growing more absent-minded. She'd leave the house with the bathtub water running. She'd pay for groceries and forget them at the store. She'd search all over for her car keys only to find them in the car . . . with the engine still running. Back in the old days I'd spend hours looking for her G-spot. During her pregnancy I spent my days looking for her lost wallet or sunglasses. I've decided that living with a pregnant woman is like sharing your life with a living brain donor. The biggest frustration I had with my wife's lack of brain cells was that she kept forgetting what I had told her.

I wish I had some suggestions on how to deal with your wife's mental depletion. The only thing I can advise is to hide spare sets of keys all over the neighborhood, and try to get everything down in writing.

Birthing 101

Most women insist on planning things out to the smallest detail. The birth of their child is no exception. In fact, watching your wife draw out her birth plan is sure to bring back memories of planning your wedding. Your wife will obsess over every last detail while you pretend to be interested.

Where

First, she has to choose where to have the baby, the most common place being a hospital. Your wife may feel it's the best option for both her and the baby because she'll be surrounded by doctors, state-of-the-art equipment, and Class 3 narcotics.

But, if your wife is having a low-risk pregnancy without complications, she may prefer a birthing center. Birthing centers are like nice hotel rooms with comfortable beds, showers, and tubs. Throw in adult movie channels and you'll want to check in now! At a birthing center, your wife will have more control of her surroundings (she can eat when she wants, walk around, listen to music) and will be assisted by a trained midwife.

The final option is a home birth, which is good if your wife is a total control freak. There she can do as she pleases and give birth (with the aid of a midwife) while wearing her favorite flannel jammies and sprawled out on your highest thread count sheets (which you should subsequently burn).

How

Now that you got the "where" down pat, let's go over the "how." First up, there's natural birth, which means no drugs (it can be taken further to mean no medical intervention of any kind such as breaking the water, or labor-inducing medications). She can manage her pain by using Lamaze breathing or the techniques of self-hypnosis (if you want a laugh, read all about it at *www.hypnobirthing.com*).

Your wife may prefer having a water birth. As you know, women love taking baths, a concept we men don't share. The idea here is that the transition from comfy uterus to the cold cruel world is less traumatic if the baby is born into a warm, wet environment.

Finally, she could prefer the "get this thing out of me the fastest and easiest way possible" plan, which includes a smorgasbord of pain meds, labor-inducing drugs, and anything else modern medicine has invented to have a speedy and painless-as-possible delivery.

The Birth Plan

The one inherent problem with your wife's detailed birth plan, however, is that it's destined to piss her off. Mother Nature will be calling the shots on delivery day, and her plan might not agree with your wife's (remember the rain at your outdoor wedding?). Your wife may decide to give birth at home, but if there's fetal distress, it may warrant a trip to the hospital. Or she may be insistent on a vaginal delivery, but discover that the baby is breech (turned the wrong way). And no matter how much she wants a fully natural delivery, she may suffer from back labor, making labor so intense that she'll beg for drugs like Courtney Love.

As you can see, there are many reasons why your wife is lamenting over her birth plan. So many choices! You and I both know that even under the best of circumstances the birth plan might be shot to hell, but making a detailed birth plan gives your wife comfort. Even better, it keeps her busy during this long last leg of the journey. So feign your interest, and be supportive. Oh, and most important, don't laugh at that hypnobirthing crap while she's in the room!

Words You Should Know

Childbirth classes: There are a host of classes you can take, from Lamaze to hypnobirthing to those offered at your hospital and birthing centers. These go over the basics of delivery, from how to time out contractions to how you can help your wife to how to cut the cord. I highly recommend them.

Doula: She's a trained labor coach who will help your wife through labor and delivery. She gives her emotional support and guides her through labor without giving any medical assistance. A doula charges anywhere from $100 to $1,000 (not covered by insurance).

Midwife: Health care providers who focus on delivering babies. There are different levels of training for midwives. Direct entry midwives are at the lowest level and aren't regulated. In fact, in some states, it's illegal for them to practice. At the highest level are certified nurse-midwives, who are qualified for home and birthing center deliveries.

They Grow Up So Fast . . . Especially in Utero

During this month, your kid has completed the construction phase of its life. All of the parts have been assembled and the final touches are being made. The lungs are developed enough for your kid to breathe on its own. Its hearing is acute enough to hear noises outside the womb. Your baby's pupils will constrict if a light is shined in its eyes. Its toenails and fingernails are formed, and even its delicate eyelashes have filled in. And, for the final touch, your child's colon has a dark tarlike substance inside that will be pooped out after birth. These days Junior keeps himself busy by sucking on his thumb and playing with his umbilical cord. By the end of this month your baby will weigh as much as a good-sized chicken—about five pounds.

9

The Ninth Month

Getting through the ninth and final month of pregnancy can be tough for both you and your wife. By now her pregnancy symptoms are at their highest level and your patience is running at its lowest. You both know that if the baby were born today it could survive fine outside the womb, it just needs to gain a little more weight. So while it packs on the pounds, you have no choice but to wait it out. You go to birthing class. You prepare the baby's room. You take a tour of the hospital. You have the baby shower. You do everything you can to kill time, and not each other.

This ninth month is also a very confusing time emotionally. You feel more excited about being a father than ever before. You're also more terrified. You're more in love with your wife than you ever thought possible. And she's also bugging the hell out of you. This month seems to drag on forever.

As if you're not stressed enough, you're barraged by endless phone calls from well-meaning yet totally irritating friends and family. They want up-to-the-minute reports on your wife's dilation and contraction count as if it were the

Dow Jones average after the housing crash. Yes, this ninth
and final month is definitely a hard one to persevere through.
So while you wait for the bough to break, take a moment
to finish up learning about this last rung on the pregnancy
ladder.

What Goodies Await You This Month

By now your wife has had every ailment in the book. She's
been there, done that. The only new symptom that she'll
experience this month is the overwhelming desire to get the
kid out of her. So, instead of repeating myself about what
kind of misery to expect, I thought I'd fill you in on how to
tell the difference between false labor and the real thing.

False labor is fairly common during the ninth month.
By now the pain of Braxton-Hicks is in full swing and it
can easily be mistaken for the onset of labor. Also, every
little contraction that your wife will have could be perceived as the key that will finally unlock her from the
prison of pregnancy, and she reads more into it than she
should. My wife had a case of false labor. She woke me up
in the middle of the night to tell me that she was in labor,
and I bolted out of bed. I was filled with adrenaline and
ready to rock and roll, but in less than an hour her contractions stopped. So, instead of having a baby that night,
all I had was insomnia.

In hopes of sparing you a sleepless night or a false run to
the hospital, I'll explain some of the ways that you can dif-
ferentiate between false labor and the real enchilada.

False Labor
- Contractions aren't regular.
- Pain is in the lower belly rather than the lower back.
- Baby kicks strongly during contractions.
- Contractions slow down if you change positions or walk around.

Real Labor
- Pain is in lower back, then spreads to lower stomach or legs.
- Your wife may have diarrhea or become nauseated.
- Contractions become worse and more frequent as time goes by.
- Water breaks (this only happens for about 15 percent of women).
- Your wife has a red or pink discharge (called "show").

The Push Gift

The push gift is what men call the bauble that they're expected to give to their wives after the baby is born. Personally, I think it's a ridiculous tradition. To begin with, the whole reasoning behind the push gift is warped. Women feel that they should have some kind of marker to remember this special day. They do. It's called their kid. Second, a push gift is a total waste of money. Here you are in the biggest financial crunch of your life and you're expected to spend a fortune on a stupid bauble. Wouldn't it be more prudent to put the money aside for your kid's college education?

You may think I sound bitter. Well, maybe I am. And maybe I'm feeling just a little bit jealous, too. Why aren't there push gifts for men? Sure, we don't do the actual pushing, but God knows that we've suffered through labor pains in our own special way. Where's our big-screen TV? Our band saw? Our nine iron? These push gifts are just another way to show men that they really aren't an important and integral part of the pregnancy experience.

That said, if your wife is the kind of woman who will expect some sort of trinket on the big day (and what woman isn't), maybe I can be of some help. I'm not much of a shopper, but I have learned one important thing: The most essential aspect to this push gift is that it be sentimental. Therefore, no toaster ovens or bread warmers, please. Some of the best suggestions that I can offer you are:

1. **A charm bracelet with a charm representing the baby**— maybe a little shoe or a heart with room for an inscription of the baby's name and birth date. This gift will come in handy later on, for it takes the guesswork out of what to get your wife every Mother's Day. If you have a charm bracelet, you can simply add a new charm to it every year. The most sentimental part of this gift is that if you have a daughter, you can pass it on to her when she's grown up.

2. **A cameo is another good gift,** especially a cameo that has an etching of a mother and her child. You can find them in antiques shops, jewelry stores, and even on the Internet.

3. **A ring with the baby's birthstone is a good idea.** It may be tricky to know in advance what your kid's birthstone might be, but you'll come pretty close if you

follow your wife's due date. If your baby chooses to ignore doctor's orders and be born premature or weeks late, you can probably have the stone swapped out.

Birthstones:
- **January:** garnet or rose quartz
- **February:** amethyst or onyx
- **March:** aquamarine or bloodstone
- **April:** diamond or rock crystal (quartz)
- **May:** emerald or chrysoprase
- **June:** alexandrite or moonstone or pearl
- **July:** ruby or carnelian
- **August:** peridot or sardonyx
- **September:** sapphire or lapis
- **October:** opal or tourmaline
- **November:** topaz or citrine
- **December:** zircon or turquoise

4. **Lockets also make great push gifts.** You could put a photo of yourself in one side and leave the other side reserved for one of your baby.
5. **If you're turned off to the whole bejeweled thing, a spa day would be greatly appreciated.**
6. **If money is tight, you can always go for the "awww" gift of a cute teddy bear or a beautiful flower arrangement.** Women just melt when you remember their favorite flower.
7. **A certificate good for a month with a housekeeper or baby nurse.** You could arrange for a food delivery service. Or you could give her a coupon good for diaper changes or running errands or getting up with the baby at night.

If you're against the idea of the push gift and want to forget the whole thing entirely, go right ahead. By doing so you may start a trend and rid the human race of this unworthy tradition. Maybe it will make your wife realize that by far, the greatest and most cherished gift that you can give her after she gives birth to your child is your unconditional love and support. Yeah, right. That'll go over real big.

How to Pamper Your Preggo

When my wife was pregnant, she would compare the last trimester of pregnancy to skiing. If you've ever been on the slopes then you know from where she speaks. You understand how difficult it can be to perform even the simplest of tasks when you're in full ski attire. Walking becomes a chore when wearing heavy boots. Bending over is impossible in those bulky down parkas. And putting on socks requires more endurance than Rob Lowe needed to make that infamous sex video.

After a day of just doing the simple routine things required to live, my wife's back would ache, her feet would swell, and she'd perspire like, well, like Rob Lowe did when making that infamous sex video. I realized that if there was ever a time when my wife needed to be pampered, this was definitely it. But what could I do to indulge her? How could I heal her wounded body and boost her sagging spirits? After doing a little research I found a few things that did the trick:

1. **Get her a coupon for a pregnancy massage.** Most major spas offer them. They're similar to a regular massage but the tables have a hole cut out in the center. This

way your wife can lie down on her stomach for the first time in months. In addition, these massages focus on the problems of a preggo, like sciatica and backache.

2. **Get your wife a home foot spa.** They're like little hot tubs for the feet. You add hot water and turn on the vibrating action and watch your wife oooh and ahhh her troubles away.

3. **Take your wife swimming.** The water takes the weight off of her stomach and it gives her body a well-deserved break from having to carry itself around all day.

4. **Buy a pregnancy mattress.** It's a large foam pad with a hole cut out of the center so that your wife can sleep on her stomach. It you can't afford that, go to the beach and dig a hole in the sand. Either way, she's going to love it.

5. **Get her a gift certificate for a pedicure.** Most pregnant women neglect their feet, since they can't even see them. Not only will a pedicure feel great, but you'll appreciate it, too. No longer will her feet look like those of your grandfather.

6. **Indulge her in her favorite pregnancy food.** I got my wife a year's worth of the Fruit of the Month Club. It's delicious, healthy, and every month it gave her a new option of something to throw at me.

You may be able to think of several different things depending on what your wife likes. If she likes flowers, get her flowers. If she has a favorite author, buy her the author's latest book. Just do something to show her that you care. I know that after all these months of abuse you deserve some pampering to, but do something for her. It really is a win-win situation. When she's pampered, she'll be relaxed, happy, and grateful, which is just the way you want her to be. Of course, her happiness will only last until her next sciatica pain, but it'll still be worth every penny.

The Baby Shower

About this time you'll discover a wonderful way to get oodles of baby goodies without even spending a dime. It's due to that great invention called a baby shower. Women started this tradition generations ago to offer support to the mother-to-be, to share child-rearing secrets, and to "shower" her with baby necessities to make the job easier. In addition to giving your wife the feeling of womanly kinship, this event can also save you a crapload of cash.

If you register right, you won't have to purchase baby items for almost a year after the baby's born. But most couples make one crucial mistake when registering. They forget that their baby is going to grow up. They only envision it as a newborn and forget that it will need many additional items during the months ahead. For instance, did you know that your little one is going to grow so much during its first year, that she'll need a completely new wardrobe every three months? Therefore, make sure that you request clothing in various sizes.

Consider registering for educational toys that help teach your baby important things like lifting its head, sitting up, and crawling. There are also swings and jumpers that fit under doorjambs that should keep your baby entertained long enough for you to check out the scores.

Handy Man

There's a reason why men aren't invited to most baby showers. It's so they can store up their energy to prepare them for the ordeal of assembling the onslaught of gifts. After my wife's baby shower, she was in awe of the generosity of her family and friends. I, on the other hand, was in awe of the pile of stuff that I had to put together.

Some of the items that will need your attention after your wife's shower are as follows:

- The baby's crib
- The bassinet
- The changing table
- The stroller
- The mobile
- The high chair
- The battery-operated swing
- The playpen
- The car seat (you don't have to assemble it, but you do have to install it into your car; often local hospitals or police departments will have clinics showing you the proper way to install yours, as they are often incorrectly installed)
- The exercise saucer

This list may make you a bit nervous, especially if you're the kind of man who has trouble swapping out the batteries in your remote control. But having a kid will teach you many things. You'll learn to be patient. You'll learn to be less self-centered. And you'll learn how to become a good handyman. Once your wife enters the final stages of pregnancy, your fix-it skills are going to be honed as sharp as a bowie knife. That's because many baby items do not come preassembled, which leaves you very few choices. Since most women feel that growing the child in their belly is about all the construction they're willing to do, putting together the baby stuff will be your responsibility. You can hire someone to do it for you; ask someone for help, preferably a friend whom you've recently helped move; or you can learn how to do it yourself.

If you choose the last of these, prepare yourself for some stressful times ahead; you'll find that "some assembly required" means a long list of instructions and many parts.

It doesn't seem fair really. Women get support throughout every aspect of pregnancy. There are ample books to read, their own personal doctors to guide them through, even classes to teach them the most fundamental basics like how to dilate. But when it comes to putting together baby items, men have to fend for themselves. There should be a special baby class for men where they learn things like how to connect part A with part B.

I'm not sure why baby items are so hard to assemble. Maybe inflicting men with this mental anguish is God's way of evening out the whole childbirth thing. But if you know a couple of basic rules, it may make your labor less laborious.

- **Before you begin any project, make sure that the package includes all the parts you'll need to build whatever it is that you're building.** There's usually a parts list on the first page of the instruction manual that specifies how many nuts and bolts are included in the box. If your package is missing even one screw, then you're screwed.

- **Make sure that you have the tools needed to assemble your project.** Again, on the instructions is a list of every hammer, screwdriver, and wrench you'll need to construct your project. If you're short a few things, don't stress. That's why God invented neighbors.
- **Don't try to save time by skipping instructions.** I know I've been guilty of this myself. I didn't think it necessary to do every minute detail, and I was sure I knew better than the manufacturers. Turns out, I didn't.
- **Test-drive your final product.** Once you finish the job, put an item of the approximate weight of your child inside of it and go for a spin. This way in case a wheel falls off or the thing comes crashing to the floor, you know you've spared your kid some pain and yourself the anguish of trying to explain to your wife what happened to the baby.

If, after my insightful words of wisdom, you're still having problems, look at the instructions to see if there's a website you can go to for help. Or see if you can find a hotline number where you can speak with an actual living person. I know that the handyman skill won't come easy, but after assembling a few hundred baby items, you should consider yourself a pro. You may even get motivated to tackle the more complex household tasks, like changing out the dirty air-conditioner filter.

Guess Who's Coming to the Delivery Room?

Not every couple has the same idea about who will be coming into the delivery room. Some women see childbirth as an intimate experience shared by husband and wife, while others see it as an excuse for a family reunion. It's a good idea to discuss your viewpoint ahead of time so that both parties can speak their minds, and make sure there are enough chairs for the guests in the room.

Today, it's so common to have a room full of guests that a couple may be perceived as selfish if they want to experience this alone (or at least alone with half a dozen medical personnel).

If you and your wife don't agree about the guest list at this soiree, you're probably out of luck. In most households, it's the wives who are in charge of planning the family's comings and goings, especially if the coming is something coming out of her. Besides, there is one benefit to having extra people in the room: your wife will have so many other options when she needs someone to yell at.

Must-Have Things for the Delivery Room

At some point during the ninth month, you and your wife will pack a bag to take to the hospital. Since this is your first experience doing so, you'll probably overpack. Your wife will have an endless list of supplies that she feels she must take for the trip. She'll bring her makeup case, her hair products, and a comfy nightie that she'll never get to wear unless she wants it tie-dyed with bodily fluids. She'll bring a familiar object from home to focus on during a contraction, and some magazines to read. Her suitcase will be packed like she's headed off to the Four Seasons for the weekend.

When it comes to the fathers, they usually do one of two things. They either overpack, and decide to bring a laptop, a good book, an iPod, a cooler, and a small TV so they won't miss whatever important game is on, or they take nothing, keeping with the attitude that the day is all about their wives.

Having been through it before, I feel that the proper way to pack is somewhere in between. Sure, labor may take a while, especially if it's the first time, but even so, you won't have much free time to lounge around. My advice? Take the following and leave your laptop at home.

1. **Camera.** Whether it's a video camera or a still, you'll want to take photos of this amazing day. Remember to pack any power cords, memory cards, or other necessities that go along with them.

2. **Toiletries for yourself as well as your wife.** You'll want to look your best for all the photo ops, and you don't want to greet your child for the first time with morning breath.

3. **An extra set of comfortable clothes.** You may come to the hospital straight from work and want to change into something more comfortable.

4. **Some snacks.** I don't know what will happen with you, but my wife didn't want me to leave the room for even a second and miss out on one contraction. It's not so much that she wanted me to be there to experience the entire birth, it's that she wanted me close by so that she'd have someone to call names. This made sneaking out to the hospital cafeteria pretty much a no-can-do. So, instead of nibbling on ice chips for hours on end, have some snacks on hand.

5. **A cell phone.** Not all hospitals have in-room calling. This is something that you should check into if you take a tour of the hospital.

6. **The "to-call" list.** Finally, take along a phone list so that you have the numbers of friends and family members with whom you want to share the good news.

Although it's not something you can pack in your overnight bag, you may want to keep a sleeping bag in the trunk of your car in case you're planning on sleeping at the hospital. True, most hospitals do provide sleeping arrangements in the room for the new dad, but you may find a sleeping bag more comfortable. Also, make sure that you keep your car filled up with gas during the ninth month.

How to Stimulate Labor

By now you're both pretty much done with the pregnancy thing. What was once a time of great delight is now a time of great despair. Your wife is so big that she's afraid that she'll rip in half, and you want your old nonpregnant wife back. By now your little one has overstayed his welcome and it's time for it to get going. But how can you get the kid to come on out?

At some point during the ninth month, you'll try to get labor started. Technically the kid is ready to come out anyway. By the time the ninth month rolls around all the crucial parts are in place in order for it to perform its required duties of crying, eating, and pooping.

My wife and I tried everything in the book to get our daughter out. I can't really say that anything worked for us. We just had to wait it out like a prisoner doing hard time. But if you want to give it a go, here's the list of all the possible ways to induce labor that have been discovered by the old wives and modern medicine.

1. **Have sex.** This is the only way to start labor that's based on medical fact. It seems that there are prostaglandins in seminal fluid that are known to cause cramping. Technically, you don't even have to take the time to please your wife, since all she needs is to lock in your juices.

2. **Eat spicy food.** Although not medically proven, this can be a rather tasty way to start things off. You may want to avoid this method if your wife has heartburn, which, at this late stage, is probably 100 percent of all pregnant women.

3. **Take a walk with your wife.** Even if this doesn't work, at least you've killed a few minutes.

4. **Eat "The Salad" that is reputed to induce labor.** This salad has been talked about for years through the pregnancy grapevine. It's served at a restaurant called Caioti in Studio City, California. I'm told that the secret ingredient is in the balsamic dressing, and they can ship this dressing anywhere. My wife and I ate there during our ninth month and, true to its word, my wife did go into labor. Of course, it took about two weeks for her to do so, but eventually, labor did take place.

I know that you may not believe me, but I promise you that one day soon your kid will finally get out of its womb. And once it does, you won't have to face this kind of challenge for another eighteen years. By then he'll be so scared to face the world again that you'll have trouble getting him out then as well. Of course the list of things that you can do to evict him will be different, but your desire to do so will be just as strong.

The Light at the End of the Birth Canal

During this ninth month, it's common for women to experience prelabor symptoms that will mark the beginning of the end. Here are some of the most common symptoms that will make you both jump for joy.

1. **Unbeknownst to you, your wife has grown a mucus plug,** a corklike thing in her cervix to protect the baby from infection. But, because her cervix is starting to dilate, this mucus plug is starting to loosen and may fall out when she goes to the bathroom.
2. **Your wife may feel more pressure in her pelvis as the baby drops lower.**
3. **She may get a persistent backache.**
4. **She may become nauseated and even throw up.** This is Mother Nature's way of getting her to slow down on the chow. Her body may need to concentrate on getting the baby out, not digesting a ham sandwich.
5. **Your wife may start to clean everything in sight.** This is referred to as the "nesting instinct" and is quite common in the ninth month. I suggest that you take full advantage of it and have her wax your car.
6. **Your wife may have a bloody discharge called "show."**
7. **She may have more Braxton-Hicks than before** and they may get more painful.
8. **She may have diarrhea during the last few days,** and may even lose a few pounds.

If your wife is having any one of these symptoms, it may just mean that her pregnancy is coming to an end. Her cervix, like a highly anticipated Broadway play, will finally be making its grand opening.

They Grow Up So Fast . . . Especially in Utero

Your baby has gained about a half to three-quarters of a pound every week during this last month. It will start to drop into your wife's pelvis, which can make her breathing a little easier. Its umbilical cord is about 20 inches long and will keep supporting your kid through delivery until the lungs take over the job of breathing. The thick cheesy coating of vernix that covers your baby is going away. Your kid's heels now have creases. This may not mean anything to you, but it's a sign that your baby has reached fetal maturity. Don't be surprised, though, if Junior decides to get a late checkout time from the womb. It's very common for a baby to be born after its due date.

10

Thar She Blows!

When my wife remembers the day that she delivered our daughter, she thinks of the opening from Charles Dickens's classic *A Tale of Two Cities*: "It was the best of times. It was the worst of times." The "best" part is obvious. She was finally a mommy and had a beautiful baby girl. But it was also the worst of times because of the drama surrounding that day.

The first horror was the enormous amount of pain that she had to go through. She dilated from 1 centimeter to 10 in only an hour and a half. She was the Mario Andretti of dilation. But unfortunately, by the time the doctor arrived, she wasn't allowed to have an epidural since they have to be administered before getting to 10 centimeters.

The next saga was that they couldn't get our baby out, and both mother and daughter (and I) were showing signs of distress. After hours of pushing, our daughter was still refusing to make her grand appearance. Was she too big? Was my wife too small? No one knew. All they did know was that the baby was stuck. Finally, in a last-ditch effort, they were able to vacuum her out on the last try before they would have had to proceed to do a cesarean.

You may think that we were the exception, and that your delivery will be drama-free. Maybe you're right. Maybe you'll be one of the lucky ones. Perhaps your wife will be given ice chips and an epidural and will nap the day away while you watch hours of uninterrupted ESPN. But statistics show that there's a much bigger chance that there'll be some drama in store for you as well. Maybe your baby will be in a breech position. Maybe your wife will have back labor. Maybe the epidural will go up too high and your wife will feel like she's having trouble breathing. The plot twists are endless.

I hope that your delivery is short, uncomplicated, and includes an epidural (as much to alleviate your discomfort as your wife's). But if it's not, realize that you're in good company, and that once it's over with, you'll have a much more exciting story to tell to your kid one day.

Stage Fright

Since we all know you didn't pay much attention in birthing class, let me explain the basics to you. Labor is divided into three separate stages. Although each stage has its own specific name, I like to refer to them as:

1. I hate you!
2. Get this thing out of me, for God's sake!
3. Thank God that's over!

The way these various stages are defined are as follows.

Stage One: I Hate You!

Stage one is actually broken down into three separate phases. The first phase is known as early labor. This could last from several hours to several days as your wife's cervix dilates to 3 centimeters. During this time you can expect your wife to be excited, nervous, and maybe a bit cranky when a contraction hits. But her contractions should be few and far between and so will your involvement. At this point, all you're expected to do is time the contractions and get to the hospital when they're about five minutes apart (maybe sooner than that, depending on how far you live from the hospital and what the traffic is like).

The next phase is known as active labor, because this is when all the action takes place. As your wife dilates from 3 to 7 centimeters, she'll be throwing things, yelling and screaming, and acting like a crazed animal. And you will be her prey. You can try to massage her, count her through contractions, and hold her hand, but chances are she won't want you to touch her in any way, and even the sound of your voice may set her off into a rage.

Phase three is called the transition phase, because this is when your private delivery room transitions into Grand Central Station. Various nurses and medical staff arrive, setting up warming lights and other equipment. Your wife's contractions are almost on top of one another, as are her insults and your inflicted injuries. This last phase usually takes less than an hour as your wife fully dilates, but to you it will seem like an eternity—a very loud, painful, stressful, helpless eternity.

Stage Two: Get This Thing out of Me, for God's sake!

Now comes the good part. It's time for your wife to push. And what makes it even better is that the doctor finally arrives, which, for some magical reason, makes your wife stop yelling at you. After all is said and done, it turns out to be a good thing that your wife has a crush on her doctor. During the pushing stage, you may have to hold on to your wife's leg or lift up her head for support, but this part is pretty much a cakewalk for you. Your wife, on the other hand, will be in hell.

Stage Three: Thank God That's Over!

The baby is out! And as soon as the baby is pushed out, your wife's contractions subside and she's as happy as she's ever been in her life. And even though the doctor may be delivering the placenta or stitching up her vagina due to a tear or an episiotomy, your wife won't even notice. Both you and your wife will cry and embrace, and all of the cruel things that she inflicted upon you will be instantly forgiven.

How to Be a Good Coach

You know that your presence in the delivery room really isn't necessary. The truth is that your wife will have the baby with or without you, and being there won't affect the outcome one little bit. It won't influence the intensity of her contractions, the amount of pushing needed, or how much the baby will weigh. In fact, the only reason that your wife wants you with her at all is that she's been told by so-called "experts" that she needs you as her labor coach. Since it's your kid that she's having, you figure it's the least you can do. Besides, you've had years of experience with coaches from Little League through high school PE, so you feel qualified for the job.

You get in the game and try to do your best. You count her breathing and time her contractions. You massage her back and try to get her to relax. You run for supplies like ice chips, juice, and washcloths. But then it hits you, or actually she does after you've rubbed her in the wrong spot, and you realize that you suck at this coaching stuff. You're not taking her pain away, and you seem to be upsetting her more than you're helping. You're not even sure why they call it a "coach" to begin with. You've had plenty of coaches in your day and not once did you ever turn to them and yell, "Shut up, jerkwad! If you think you can do a better job than I can, then you do it yourself!"

If you have high hopes of being a great labor coach, I'm afraid that I'll have to burst your bubble. Let me tell you what being a true labor coach really entails.

The Job Duties of a Labor Coach

1. **Be there so she'll have someone to curse at.** It doesn't matter how small the infraction, she's going to get angry at you. My wife's still upset at me because I made her get up off the floor during a contraction. She was blocking the hallway, for God's sake.

2. **Be available so she'll have someone to inflict pain on.** When one of her contractions hits, you need to be close by so she can dig her nails into you, squeeze your hand into pulp, or pull out whatever is left of your hair.

3. **Be there so she'll have someone to blame.** You have to cut her a little slack on this one because she's right. She's writhing in pain because nine months ago, you caught a glimpse of her bending over to unload the dishwasher.

4. **Be there so she'll have someone to belittle and demean.**

So if you have aspirations of being the Bear Bryant of labor coaches, let me give you a little inspiration. It's not whether you win or lose, it's if you can get out of there alive!

Your Labor Pains

Your wife has it good during labor. I know most people don't see it that way, but it's true. Sure, she's in a lot of pain. But it's nothing compared to the pain that you're going through. At least she's being hospitalized for hers. She has nurses to dote on her, a bed to relax in, a room full of friends and family who wait on her every need. And of course, an anesthesiologist to give her drugs that addicts would die for.

But what about you? Who's there to take away your pain? Where are your doting nurses and painkillers? People don't seem to realize that fathers are patients, too. Granted, your wife's nauseated, but you are having hunger pains because you haven't eaten for so long. Your muscles are aching from trying to hold up your linebacker-sized wife while she's breathing. Your wrist is snapped in two because she twisted it so hard during that last contraction. And you stand alone and suffer deep humiliation as she calls you every name in the book.

As usual, you can never complain about what you have to go through. Not once can you utter a single word about your exhaustion or your feelings of helplessness. Once again it's all about her, her, her! In fact, if you do ever gripe, you're criticized and blamed for being insensitive and self-centered. Where is the justice?

When will medical science realize that we laboring fathers need assistance, too? If I had my way, there would be a mini-bar set up in every delivery room across the country. There would be a physical therapist on duty to rub the pinched nerves in our necks due to all the stress. And there would be a nearby suture room to repair the scrapes and bruises inflicted upon us by our wives' flailing arms and extra-long pregnancy nails. This practice of seeing only the woman as a patient is more inhumane than animal testing, and even lab rats have a group of supporters trying to change that policy. As soon as there's a politician running for office who supports the minibar thing, he will definitely get my vote.

The Bitch Is Back

No matter what the personal dynamics you have with your wife at home, things will change when you get to the delivery room. Maybe your wife is meek and mild-mannered. Maybe she never instigates fights with you because she hates confrontations. Well, all that is about to change.

Of course, things won't be as bad if your wife wants an epidural. But don't be under the delusion that anesthesiologists are like waiters at a four-star restaurant. They don't just come whenever you snap your fingers. Often they're busy with other patients or working other floors. And in order to even get an epidural, your wife has to meet their minimum dilation requirements but not exceed their maximum ones.

If she's only at 1 or 2 centimeters, the only thing the hospital will give her is their sympathy. If your wife decides to skip the epidural and have a natural childbirth like a prairie woman, I feel for you. I know what it's like to have to suffer that kind of abuse.

Normally my wife and I get along fairly well. Sure, we have our differences, mainly when it comes to the setting on the thermostat, but at the hospital, she turned into another woman entirely. She hated everything about me: the way I looked, the way I talked, even the way I breathed. I made some kind of noise when I breathed that only she and stray dogs could hear. And she yelled at me with every breath I took.

My only advice is to take it like the man that you are. Don't pick a fight or yell back. You should also keep an eye on the monitor. You'll know before she will when a contraction will subside. But until it does, stay calm and count to ten. It may help to remember that your wife is feeling pretty scared. She's the one who's trapped in a painful body, helpless to stop the pain. And if that doesn't do the trick, keep in mind that if it weren't for you and your manly needs, she never would have gotten into this predicament in the first place. Anyway, how can you forget it? She reminds you of it every ten minutes.

Birth Day Surprises

As much as you can prepare yourself for the day that your baby is born, there will still be plenty of surprises in store for you on the actual day. You may think that you know it all. You've passed your birthing class. You've watched babies be delivered on TV shows. You've listened to your wife go on ad nauseum about every minute detail. But when the big day finally arrives, there will still be some things to learn.

In a last-ditch effort to know all there is to know, let me fill you in on a few surprises that may be in store for you on this very important day.

1. **You may be surprised by how long it takes to actually push out a kid.** Whenever you've seen it on TV, it neatly takes place in between commercial breaks. But in reality, it can take as long as three hours. That is, it can take that long when it's the first kid. By the time the next one comes along, your wife can probably get it out of her with one good sneeze.

2. **You may be surprised by how much pain there is.** If your wife decides not to get an epidural, which many of them do for some asinine reason, you'll realize why they created the expression "out of your mind with pain."

3. **You may be surprised by how uninhibited your wife is about showing her naked body to strangers.** There'll be times when she's spread out like a fine buffet, and she doesn't seem to care.

4. **You may be surprised to learn that your wife may actually take a dump on the delivery room table.** About half of women do. If this kind of delivery happens, you should keep your mouth shut about it for the rest of your life.

5. **You might be surprised to learn that your kid can take a dump too, while it's still inside the womb.** If, when the water breaks, it's a greenish-brown color instead of clear, it's because your kid has taken his first poop.

6. **You may be surprised when you cut the umbilical cord to find that it has the same consistency as calamari.**

7. **You may be surprised to know that if your wife tore during the delivery or had an episiotomy,** the doctor can add an additional "husband stitch," which tightens her back up like shrink wrap.

8. **You may be surprised how pregnant your wife looks even after she gives birth.** I thought the pudge would immediately go down afterward, but it takes several weeks or even months for her uterus to shrink back to size.

Post-Delivery Stress Disorder

If I had my way, we would all go back to the way things were just a few generations ago, like in the show *Mad Men*. Back then, men paced in the waiting room (or even went to work!), oblivious to the details of how a baby actually came out. Afterward they lit a fine cigar and passed them out to their friends and family. For when it comes to childbirth, ignorance truly is bliss. Witnessing a woman deliver a baby can be a life-altering experience in both a good way and a bad, and once you've traveled through that door, you come out a different man.

On the good side, you'll have a whole new respect for your wife, maybe even for all of womankind. When you see firsthand their incredible strength as they overcome enormous pain and fear, you can't help but see them differently. It makes you realize just how beautiful they truly are. It also makes you wonder why they have such trouble opening up a jar of mayonnaise.

But even though you're inspired by the birth, you may also be disgusted by it, too. Your wife will emit more bodily fluids than you knew a body had and her vagina may need to be cut up like deli meat to allow more room for the baby to pass through. And then, just when you thought the worst was over, she'll push out a placenta that looks like piece of rotten liver.

Because of this visual display, you may never look at your wife as the sexual creature you did in the past. Weeks from now, when you can finally have sex again, you may experience flashbacks of the birth, not unlike a veteran remembering a battle. If this happens, there's only one thing to do: Start dating again. No, no, not with other women, mind you, but with your wife. Get a babysitter and plan a weekly date night. In order to picture her anew, you'll need to start the courtship process all over again. Make sure that you shave and put on cologne, and take her to a candlelit restaurant. You'll find that your stomach will twitter with excitement just as it did when the two of you first met. Having a weekly date night does wonders for regaining the healthy image of your wife once again.

If you suspect that you may be squeamish about going near your wife's genitals after seeing a baby emerge from there, watch the birth from your wife's perspective, from the head of the table. Up there you can witness the birth from a G-rated seat (okay, maybe PG-13, due to strong language). And don't feel unmanly or wimpish about how you feel. I bet if your wife caught a glimpse of herself during delivery, she'd never want to play with herself again either.

A Face That Even a Father Could Love

And then it happens. Your child is born. Until you see it live and in person, you have no idea what it's really like.

Watching our daughter being born was the most incredible thing I had ever seen in my life. I'm trying to think of the words to describe it, but I'm at a loss. (Maybe the Eskimos have one, since they have a much more descriptive language. They have about a dozen words just for a cloud!) If you can think of childbirth as a combination of discovering religion, having sex for the first time, and the taste of a great porterhouse steak, maybe you'll get a rough idea.

But brace yourself. You may be in for a shock when you see your baby for the first time. Realize that for months, he's been soaking in amniotic fluid, the same fluid that he's been peeing in. And he's spent the last several hours smushed up in a tight birth canal. Because of this, he may not look his best. His head may remind you so much of that old *Saturday Night Live* sketch, the Coneheads, that you might consider naming him Beldar. He may still be covered with that white cheesy coating. And he very well may have hair covering most of his body. His eyes may be puffy and his skin may be riddled with birthmarks. And prepare yourself before looking at his genitals. They may be red and swollen like a monkey's butt. The baby's nipples may be oozing a pinkish discharge. And if your baby's a girl, her vagina may be secreting something milky white or blood-tinged. But even though your baby looks like it's been ridden hard and put away wet, you'll still think that your bundle of joy is the most beautiful baby ever born. And you know what? It will be.

11

Home Sweet Hell

Having a child made me realize one thing: that as over-whelming and difficult as it was to endure the pregnancy process, it was nothing compared to life with a newborn. As we've discussed throughout this book, people have delusions about how joyous pregnancy can be. That same delusion continues on when you bring the baby home.

The first three months can be the hardest months of all in the child-rearing process. By far it's the most difficult adjustment period. This may come as a surprise to those who think how blissful their lives will be once the baby's home. Of course, in many ways it *will* be blissful. After all the hard work and waiting, you finally get to hold the baby you've been dreaming of. He's cute and snuggly and smells better than barbecue sauce. He coos and wiggles and makes you realize what you've been put on this planet to do.

But your little bundle of joy can also be very trying. He cries a lot and doesn't sleep when you want him to. And even though he only weighs in at a few pounds, he has more needs than your wife did during all of her pregnancy. At any given moment, your kid will need to be fed or washed or wiped or held. His fingernails will need to be clipped and his bellybutton stub will need to be cleaned out. And since he doesn't come with an "off" switch and doesn't have any batteries to wear out, there are no breaks. There's no downtime at all, not even a federal holiday to provide for the rest that you so desperately need.

So be prepared and be realistic. If you imagine that all you're going to do now that your baby is home is stare at him all day in amazement, you may be in for a rude awakening. But I feel it's my job to give you the inside look at what can happen now that the gestation stage is finally over.

What Goodies Await You after the Baby Comes Home

Just because your wife is home from the hospital doesn't mean that you don't need to help her feel better any more. Even though she may no longer be with child, she's still with aches and pains. The amount of her discomfort will usually depend on what type of delivery she had. If she had a vaginal birth without any tearing, her recovery will be the fastest. If she had an episiotomy or a tear, she'll have more difficulty walking and sitting. And if she needed a cesarean section, she may be spending more time in bed than your baby.

Her Symptoms and What You Can Do about Them

As before, you can't take the pain away. That can only take place with time and a good vial of prescription medication. But you can help to make her more comfortable.

Exhaustion
- Help out whenever possible.
- Take care of the baby so that she can take a nap.

Extreme Sweating
This can last up to several weeks after delivery, and is just her body's way of getting rid of excess fluids left over from her pregnancy.
- Make sure that she drinks plenty of water.
- Place a towel on her bed to absorb the sweat while she sleeps.
- Put on a wetsuit before giving her a hug.

Cramping
- Ask her doctor if she can take a mild pain reliever.
- Give her a heating pad for her to use on her stomach.

Heavy Vaginal Bleeding
Your wife will bleed for several weeks after delivery. And, since she probably won't be able to drive for a couple of weeks, make sure that she has enough supplies on hand. By now you should be a pro at getting these embarrassing items. This bleeding is normal and should only be a concern if it's still bright red four days after delivery, or is accompanied by a foul odor, fever, or chills.

Enormous Engorged Breasts When Her Milk Comes In
- Enjoy!
- If her breasts get too painful, advise her to take a warm shower or to apply a warm compress to her breasts (you can heat a dampened washcloth in the

microwave). If that doesn't work, have her apply an
ice pack or a bag of frozen peas to her breasts.

Black or Bloodshot Eyes from Pushing; Bruising on Her Face or Chest

- Apply a cold compress for ten minutes at a time several times a day.
- Don't let her get near a mirror.

Cracked Nipples if Breastfeeding

- Apply lanolin to the affected area. You can find this
at drugstores.
- Check to see that the baby is putting his mouth over
her entire areola, not just the nipple.

Terrified of Her First Poop

After delivering the baby, some women are afraid of
delivering number two. They fear that they'll rip their
stitches and that it will hurt. The most important thing
you can do is to get her stool softeners and make sure that
she takes them until things get more comfortable "down
there." If sitting is a problem for her, get her a soft toilet
seat cushion.

Let's Get Ready to Rumble!

In many ways, when your wife was pregnant, it brought
the two of you closer together. You were both connected
by that miracle growing inside of her and, because you
both worked so hard to make it happen, you share a bond

that seems as strong as steel. It's a good thing, too, because now that the kid is out, that bond will be tested and you will become the crash dummy. If you thought that carrying your new bride across the threshold changed your life, wait until you see how much your life changes after carrying your baby over it.

Keep in mind that both you and your wife will be stressed as you adjust to having a baby in the house. You'll be severely sleep-deprived and there will be an endless list of chores to do to satisfy your baby's needs. Your house may be full of visitors and overnight guests. On top of that, your wife will still be hormonal as her body adjusts to no longer being pregnant. If she's breastfeeding, she'll be exhausted by her endless, all-day and all-night nursing session.

Because of all of these things, there may be tension. And when there's tension there may also be fighting. During the first few months our biggest source of arguments stemmed from the fact that my wife thought she knew everything about the baby and that I wasn't doing enough to help out. Suddenly she thought that she was Dr. Spock and that I was Dr. Doing-too-little. She would correct me all the time. When I held the baby, either I wasn't supporting her head enough or I was cramping her arm too close to my side. Excuse me, but not once during the nine months that she carried the baby did I ever tell her how to do it.

Before giving birth, the only living thing that my wife ever tended to was the mold growing on our shower curtain. But our baby wasn't more than a few days old, and suddenly my wife was an expert in child development. Granted, she did know more than I did. She had already read a dozen books about how to care for a newborn. She knew the proper way to bathe the kid and could swaddle her up tighter than a burrito. And she would always throw in my face the fact that she spent years babysitting as a teenager while all I ever did was figure out how to get laid.

You may be having the same problem in your house. Maybe your wife's telling you that you're not cutting your kid's nails the way she showed you, or cleaning out its belly button stump correctly. She may be upset that the bath water you used is too hot or too cold. She may be yelling that you didn't put the right pajamas on the baby, since the ones you used have buttons in the back and the baby can feel them when it sleeps. So if the baby only takes a short nap it will be your fault. Then you get frustrated and tell her that if she's such an expert, she should do it all. And she gets more upset, accusing you of just not wanting to help out. Face it. No matter what you do, you can't win.

Another source of tension is that you may have different ideas about child rearing. One of you may think that if the baby cries, you should pick it up right away, while the other thinks it should cry a little first so it won't get spoiled. Or maybe one of you feels that the baby should sleep in its crib while the other wants it in bed with you. You'd better learn how to figure these things out now, because up until the day that your child leaves for college, there will be many issues to disagree upon, and you need to learn how to discuss them and to compromise.

Some more arguments may arise because as soon as you come home from work, your wife hands you the baby and takes off for a break. Sure, you understand that she needs some downtime after having the kid all day. But she needs to understand that you weren't down at the track all day sucking down bourbons. If you tell her how hard your day was, though, she'll get mad and start screaming about how you don't know what a hard day is until you've stayed home with a baby for hours on end.

As you can see, there are many reasons to argue. My advice is to talk about them. But do so at a time when things are calm (or some variation of that theme). Wait until the baby is asleep and you've both had some time to relax. Also, realize that most of the things you're fighting about really aren't that important in the long run. So what if you put the hooded towel on upside down after the baby's bath? So what if you sang the wrong words to the lullaby? Only argue about the things that you feel are important, and tell her to do the same. If she won't listen, hand her this book and tell her to read this section. Maybe she'll recognize that she's guilty of some of the things that I've mentioned and will ease off. Women believe everything they see in print. That's a secret that the supermarket tabloids have counted on for years.

Postpartum Sex

In most cases, sex won't even be an issue for a good six weeks after delivery. After that, your wife will return to her OB for that all-important six-week checkup. They may as well call it what it is, a sex-week checkup, because it's at that point that her doctor will probably give her the go-ahead to have sex again. By then her stitches should have healed, her bleeding should have subsided, and her cervix should be closed.

But just because the doctor tells her that sex is okay doesn't mean that you're going to get any. In fact, your wife may keep this information a secret from you for a long time. She may still feel bruised and sore from the delivery. She may be so sick and tired of things going in and out of her that she may need more time before she starts that process again.

But at some point, your wife will (probably) tell you that her doctor gave her the okay to have sex again. Sure, it may take a court-ordered subpoena to open up her medical records, but eventually she'll confess. And although you may feel as excited as a prisoner that's been granted a conjugal visit, you still have one big hurdle to overcome. You have to get her in the mood.

There will be many reasons that your wife will feel reluctant. She may be embarrassed about the extra weight that she's carrying around. She may only see herself as a mother now and think that mothers shouldn't have sex. She may be exhausted from the relentless task of taking care of a newborn. She may fear that she could get pregnant again. And after having spent all day giving to her needy child she may have nothing left to give to her needy spouse. But the biggest reason of all is that she knows that having sex again is going to hurt.

Because of this, you'll need to use your best seductive powers. You know better than I what turns your wife on, but may I suggest a scenario such as the following:

- Come home with a big bouquet of her favorite flowers.
- Help out with dinner and remember to take out the trash.
- Tell her you'll put the baby to bed that night and then actually do it.

- Give her a stiff drink—or a virgin form of her favorite if she's breastfeeding. Make sure to have all the supplies at hand in order to fix her favorite. You may need to buy a blender and some of those cute cocktail umbrellas, but have whatever you may need on hand.
- Light a fire. Even if it's in the middle of summer, light the fire. Women seem to be as drawn to them as moths. If you don't have a fireplace, use candles. If you don't have any candles, just light some matches and hope for the best.
- Put on some slow sexy music and ask her to dance.
- Make your move.

Even if you get her to this point, don't expect to get much further. That's because once you start going inside her, you won't get very far. The degree of her pain will depend on what type of delivery she had. If she had a C-section, she'll still be more or less intact, so she'll feel the least amount of pain. If she had a vaginal delivery there may be more. And finally, if she had a vaginal delivery with an episiotomy or a tear, it will hurt most of all. But even if she gave birth through her nostril, sex is still going to hurt. And, as usual, you can blame it on her hormones.

Because of these hormones (especially if she's breastfeeding) her vaginal wall will be thin and dry. It will feel as erotic as making love to an empty roll of toilet paper. Because of this, you'll need a strong lubricant and a lot of patience. I know it will be frustrating, but there's really nothing you can do.

But even if you left the event unsatisfied, at least it satisfied her curiosity about how painful sex would be. Maybe it wasn't as bad as she imagined. Maybe next time she'll relax a bit more. I promise that there will be a next time and that things will get easier. But there is one warning that I feel obligated to tell you about. If your wife is breastfeeding, you need to know that when she becomes aroused, her breasts will drip like an old faucet. Your sheets will have a wet spot that will rival that of John Holmes's. My advice is, don't let her get on top without your scuba gear.

The Shape of Things to Come

Face it, your wife's body has changed due to the pregnancy. The most obvious difference, of course, is her weight gain. And even though she's dropped a lot since she went to the hospital, she's far from where she started. Of course you don't expect her to lose this weight overnight. But you do hope that in time, it will come off.

There's a saying in the pregnancy biz when it comes to weight loss: nine months on, nine months off. Of course this isn't a hard and fast rule. Some women will naturally snap right back into shape. Others, like celebrities, snap right back too, with a little help from their personal trainers, yoga instructors, chefs, and nutritionists. But most every woman finds that she has some level of difficulty getting back into her pre-pregnancy jeans. Pregnancy can slow down the thyroid, making it more difficult for the weight to come off. Others can't seem to lose weight while they're nursing, because providing nutrition for the baby makes them so hungry. Every woman is different.

From my extensive scientific research, which consisted of asking a bunch of my friends, it seems that the more conscientious a woman was about diet and exercise before she conceived, the more she'll be afterward. If you find that your wife is complaining about her weight gain, there really is only one way to deal with it. Be supportive. Tell her not to worry. Tell her that you'll exercise together and even get a two-for-one membership at the gym. And, of course, tell you that you'll still love her no matter how much she weighs. Because the truth is, you should. Even if she does hold on to some extra pounds, you'll get your revenge one day when you go bald, lose a few teeth, and start growing hair out of your nose and ears. I promise that soon enough you'll be worse for the wear yourself, and you won't have the excuse of growing a human being inside of you to blame for it. And I assure you, when this happens, you'll want your wife to stick by you, too.

In addition to your wife's weight gain, you may notice other ways that her body looks different. And, if your wife ever lets you look at her naked again, you may notice some of these changes. Here are a few of her possible bodily changes:

- **Her vulva may sag a little bit.** It droops a bit lower than where it was before, changing her girlish figure in yet another way.
- **Her bellybutton may be a different shape.** There may be more of an overhang than before, or it may be more of an outtie.
- **If she had a tear or needed to have an episiotomy,** her vagina may not line up quite the way it lined up before.
- **Her breasts may be smaller and sag a bit more.** Also, the skin on them may become looser.

- **She may have some spider veins and varicose veins left on her legs.** Although many disappear after delivery, some tend to linger.
- **She may have stretch marks on her skin on the places that did most of the stretching,** namely her breasts and stomach.
- **She may have a small "spare tire" around her waist because of how much her skin had stretched.** And, no matter how much weight she loses or exercise she does, it may not go away.
- **She may have a few more moles than before.**

Remember that even though your wife may have emerged through pregnancy a little worse for the wear, the reason for it is well worth it. And if you ever have trouble seeing one of your wife's new battle scars, look at your baby and put it in perspective. And remember, if you look at her and don't have anything nice to say, make something up.

Postpartum Depression

It wasn't too long ago that most people knew very little about postpartum depression. Then came gruesome news stories about new moms inflicting harm on their children, and public stories about Brooke Shields's battle with the problem.

New mothers may face a few types of postpartum anxiety. The most common is called the "baby blues." Baby blues can happen right after delivery. For no apparent reason, your wife will cry, or go from happy to sad in the blink of an eye. Fortunately, the baby blues don't require any treatment except for time, an occasional hug, and some desperately needed breaks.

The next level of this condition is called "postpartum depression." This could happen a few days to even a few months after childbirth. In this case, the woman will experience feelings similar to baby blues but she'll feel them much deeper. The signs are feeling restless or sad; crying a lot; having no energy; experiencing headaches, chest pains, heart palpitations, or numbness; not being able to sleep; not eating (or overeating); having trouble remembering things and making decisions; and being overly worried or not interested in the baby. In the worst of cases, she may be afraid of hurting the baby. If your wife experiences any of these symptoms, you should take her to her health care provider to get treatment. She'll need medication and counseling. If left untreated, postpartum depression could get worse.

The most severe form of postpartum depression is called "postpartum psychosis." It often starts within the first three months after delivery. In this situation, women can lose touch with reality. They can have auditory and visual hallucinations and delusions. Other symptoms include insomnia, feeling agitated and angry, and having strange feelings and behaviors. These women need treatment right away. In some cases, they can require hospitalization to prevent risk to themselves and to others.

No one knows what causes these disorders. Many think that they're triggered by the woman's hormonal changes after delivery. When she's pregnant, her hormones greatly increase. Right after delivery, they plummet. So does her thyroid level. She's sleep-deprived and overwhelmed, and stressed out because she's not at work or works too much and has no free time.

The biggest problem you may face in helping your wife is that you may not even know that she's having any problems. Many new moms don't want to admit how they really feel. They're ashamed to. They think that they should be Supermom, up all day and night attending to their baby's every need. My wife had the blues, but I had no idea until months later. She never admitted it to anyone. So instead, I would come home from work completely unaware that she had spent most of the day stressed out and crying.

So be aware of postpartum depression and look for the signs. But realize that as hard as you may look, you may never find them. So, even if your wife appears to be handling things just fine, be extra nice and caring toward her for the first few weeks after the baby is born. Help out as much as you can and give her breaks as often as possible. And, of course, that occasional hug doesn't hurt anyone either.

Tips on Travel

When I was traveling by plane before I had a child, I'd watch the parents with screaming kids and feel sorry for them. I'd see their desperate attempts to soothe their kids' tantrums by feeding them fish-shaped crackers and pulling out an endless stream of toys from their diaper bags. The parents never said one word to each other the entire trip. They only spoke to nearby passengers to apologize profusely for the disturbance. I would sit back with my magazine and feel lucky that I wasn't one of them. I swore that if I ever had kids, I would never travel with them until they were old enough to pilot the plane.

But then, suddenly, it was me in that airplane with my wife and child. I was the one pulling out the fish-shaped crackers and the endless stream of toys. And I understood why new parents would do something as stupid as to fly across the country with their kids. The reason? Grandparents. I knew my folks back home were desperate to see their grandchild and it was up to me to get her there. So, I bought our tickets, packed our bags, and searched my medicine cabinet for anything to make the flight more enjoyable.

After several journeys there and back, I picked up a few pointers to make the plane ride more doable. So if you have parents in another state, here is my advice.

Tips for Airplane Travel

1. **Make sure to schedule your child's feedings in accordance with the plane's takeoff.** The reason that kids scream from the moment the plane takes off is because of the painful pressure in their ears. If you can, have him nurse or give him a bottle during takeoff. That should make your ride smoother from the get-go. The same holds true for the descent, but since it's much more gradual, the pressure won't be as bad.

2. **Bring bubbles.** They're easy to pack and simple to use. They don't make noise and your kid will love to watch them. I'd go to the back of the plane and blow bubbles until I thought I would faint. I never had any trouble with the flight crew and if you're lucky, it will keep your baby entertained for an entire three-minute stretch!

3. **If you can afford it, buy your kid a seat on the plane.** I know it's expensive, but with the lulling sound of the

engine, kids tend to sleep during the flight. You'll both be more comfortable if he can sleep in his car seat, rather than sprawled on your lap while you lose all feeling in your arms and legs.

4. **If you can afford it, take a direct flight.** You may think that you're saving money if you have layovers, but no amount of money is worth the aggravation of extra time in the air.

5. **Take along those fish-shaped crackers.** They really are delicious.

You'll no doubt be taking trips by automobile as well. The difficult part about car travel with a newborn is that they have to face backward during the ride. I'd cry too if I had to stare at the back of a seat for hours on end. But again, there are some tricks.

How to Make for a Better Car Ride

1. **Put up a baby mirror so that your kid can look at its reflection and think it has company.** A newborn is pretty gullible and usually falls for this one.

2. **Get him some socks that have bells or toys attached to the toes** (make them if you can't find them in a store). Newborns have reflexes that make their legs jerk around involuntarily, so if he's wearing these socks, he has a constant puppet show to entertain himself.

3. **Because most infants can't hold their bottles themselves, purchase a clamp made for this purpose.** One end attaches to the car seat and the other holds the bottle. They're flexible and will allow for your baby to drink without you having to pull over.

As your baby ages, its capacity to amuse itself will grow and your trips will become much more enjoyable. And once he or she hits the iPod stage, it should become a breeze. But until then, try to make your visits few and far between and tell your folks to get a good look at their grandchild while they can, for it may be some time until they see him or her again.

Are You Stay-at-Home-Dad Material?

It used to be that I'd go to the park and see a father with a young child and automatically assume that he was divorced and it was his day with the kid. But then I'd notice that he was wearing a wedding ring and realized that he was probably a stay-at-home dad. It seems that more and more, it's the man who decides to be the primary caregiver of the family.

Stay-at-home dads were almost unheard of a generation ago. But now that women are waiting longer to have children, they may be the ones who are more financially set. They may have a better health plan, make more money, and get more vacation time. If this is true in your case, it may make sense for you to be the one to stay at home with your child.

But it takes more than just a financial statement to decide who should take over this job. It takes a strong desire for one of you to do so. Staying at home can be the most difficult job you'll ever have and, just like any other job, you have to be qualified. Here are some questions you should ask yourself to see if you meet the basic requirements:

1. Will you feel emasculated if your wife is the one who brings home the bacon?

2. Are you willing to do domestic chores like cooking, shopping, and cleaning?
3. Do you consider yourself to be nurturing and patient? If not, are you willing to learn?
4. Are you willing to put your career on hold for a few years, and maybe give up the dream of being at the highest level of the corporate ladder?
5. If you're at work now, do you find that you ache to be at home with the baby? Do you stare at the baby's photo all day? Has your work become less significant?

My friend Chris is a stay-at-home dad to his two pre-school-aged kids. Whenever I visit, which I admit is far less frequent since he took over this job, I can barely get two words in. There isn't a moment when he's not tending to some sort of catastrophe. Either a kid fell or is hungry or has spilled something on the dog or needs to have some part of its body tended to. Strangely enough, Chris loves it (most of the time anyway), and he says that he wouldn't have it any other way. Sure, he feels strange being the only male in Mommy & Me. And it is tough when he tries to console his kids and all they want is their mommy. But it does have its rewards. He gets the gift of knowing his kids like he never would if he went to work every day. He's there to witness their miraculous "firsts." And, since he's welcome in the inner circle of other mothers, he sees a whole lot more breastfeeding than he would have at an office.

Being a stay-at-home dad isn't for everyone, but if you think that it's something you may want to look into, there are books and websites you may want to check out. Sure, you may suffer financially living off of only one paycheck, but the benefits should make it well worth it. Just ask Chris.

The Games People Play

It's nighttime. The baby's crying. You're both sound asleep—
or at least you're pretending to be. Neither of you wants to
be the one who gets up, so you both play dead. Don't feel
bad. This game of trying to outlast each other is a game
that's being played by new parents all around the world. The
problem is that, just as in nuclear war, there are no winners.
What happens is that the one who gets up is mad because he
or she knows deep down that the other one was just pretending. And the person who gets to stay in bed is feeling guilty
about being in a warm toasty bed and can't go back to sleep.
But eventually you both calm down and drift off to La La
Land, all ready to start round two in just a few short hours.

I know that to some the solution is simple. Just take
turns. But it's not as simple as it sounds. Sometimes when
the baby cries, all he needs is to be held for a moment, and
then he falls back to sleep. But other times, he'll need to be
changed, fed, and rocked for hours on end. If you wind up
getting all the tough shifts, this setup won't seem fair.

Instead, I have a better idea. Take shifts. With shifts, one
person can take the 8:00 P.M. through 2:00 A.M. shift and
the other can take the 2:00 A.M. to 8:00 A.M. shift. Of course,
the times can vary depending on what time you wake up
or put the baby down at night. But at least with this plan,
there is no guilt or resentment needed. The clock is what
determines which one of you should wake up, not the ability
to outlast each other.

I know that this idea isn't foolproof. One person may
still have a more difficult shift than the other from time to
time, and one person still may get more sleep. But I found
that I wasn't as sleep-deprived if I got at least half a night

of sleep. It was the constant up-and-down thing that was grueling on my system. And the game of pretending to be sleeping was grueling on my marriage.

You may think that if your wife is breastfeeding, you get off easy. But that's not always the case. There are still plenty of ways that your wife will want you to help out. Maybe you can get the baby out of its crib or bassinet and hand it to her in bed. Maybe you can change its diaper if it needs to be changed. Or maybe, after your wife has nursed, you can rock the baby back to sleep. And, because of the invention of the breast pump, she may be able to pump bottles during the day so that you can feed the baby during the night as well. Damn technology.

How to Save for College

It seems unfathomable that your kid, who now can't even find its thumb, will one day be going off to college. And it will be even more unfathomable how much that college is going to cost. Remember, though, that while it costs a fortune, it may actually save you money in the long run. Statistics show that if your child gets a college degree, he'll earn 80 percent more income than if he didn't, and he'll therefore drain 80 percent less of yours. And, if you play your cards right and are good with guilt, your child could end up taking care of you in your old age. So, when you save for your child's college, think of it as an educational fund and a retirement account all rolled up into one.

The trick to saving for college is to start as soon as your kid pops out. In fact, before you call any friends or family to tell them the good news, you should place a call to your financial planner. Because of the beauty of compound interest, the earlier you start saving, the less money you'll need to contribute to a college savings account each month.

When it comes to saving for college, there are several plans to choose from. One popular method is called the 529 college savings plan. The great part about this plan is that your money grows tax free and, as long as you use the money for higher education, you can withdraw the money tax free as well. As with most of these savings plans, grandparents are able to contribute, too.

Another way to go would be a prepaid tuition plan. The idea behind this type of plan is that you can pay for your child's college tuition at today's prices. You pay into the state and your money is redeemed for a college that's in that specific state. I'm not sure what happens eighteen years from now when your kid wants to go to his new girlfriend's college halfway across the country, but I'll let you cross that bridge when you get to it.

Custodial accounts are also a common way to save. In many cases, this is set up by either of your parents. Money is put into it every year, some of it tax free, and the custodian of the account (usually the parent) can withdraw funds whenever needed to spend on the child. The money is taxed upon withdrawal. Once the child is a predetermined age, the money in the account will be his or hers to spend however they see fit. Personally, I'm not a fan of this one. I know that if I had had a chunk of change when I turned eighteen or twenty-one, the last thing I would have spent it on was an advanced education.

There are other methods of saving, including the Coverdell Education Savings Account, Roth IRAs, and traditional IRAs. To learn more, check out the Internet or visit with a financial planner to see which method feels right to you. If, even after all I've told you, you still choose not to save for college, there are several alternatives. Maybe you'll qualify for financial aid. Maybe your kid can earn a full scholarship. Or maybe if you're lucky, your kid will be lazy and an underachiever, thereby saving you a fortune. One can only hope.

They Grow Up So Fast . . . from Now On

Once you get past the first three months, things should get a lot easier. After that point your child will have fallen into somewhat of a schedule, so you'll know when it's time for his nap or a feeding. This will make venturing out into the world again much more manageable. After three months, your child will sleep longer stretches at night so that you won't fall asleep at your desk during the day. By the end of three months, you'll be a pro at the whole fatherhood thing and can decipher what your baby's telling you just by the sound of his cry. After three months, your baby should be able to control his movements more, so instead of simply being a bundle of reflexes, he can deliberately reach out for you and give you a hug. He also has the amazing ability to bring you to tears with just one little smile.

At about six months your baby should be sitting up. By seven months, he may be crawling. And by the time he reaches his first birthday, he may even be able to walk. I guarantee that at some point while he's learning to take his first steps, he'll walk away from you and keep on going without looking back. It's at this moment that you'll understand just how short and precious this time is with your baby, and how important it is to savor every minute of it . . . because they really do grow up so fast.

Appendix

Resources List

The following books, websites, organizations, and other resources will provide you with plenty of information and suggestions for dealing with pregnancy, cooking, gift buying, estate planning, living with a newborn, and more.

Baby Gear

BOOKS

Fields, Denise, and Alan Fields. *Baby Bargains: Secrets to Saving 20% to 50% on Baby Furniture, Equipment, Clothes, Toys, Maternity Wear and Much, Much More!* 9th ed. (Boulder, CO: Windsor Peak Press, 2011).

RETAIL CHAINS

Babies "R" Us
www.babiesrus.com

Baby's First Year

BOOKS

Karp, Harvey. *The Happiest Baby on the Block: The New Way to Calm Crying and Help Your Baby Sleep Longer* (New York: Bantam, 2003).

Murkoff, Heidi Eisenberg, Arlene Eisenberg, and Sandee Hathaway. *What to Expect the First Year* (New York: Workman Publishing, 2009).

Nee, Tekla S. *The Everything® Baby's First Year Book: Complete Practical Advice to Get You and Baby Through the First 12 Months* (Avon, MA: Adams Media, 2010).

Childbirth

BOOKS

Ford-Martin, Paula. *The Everything® Birthing Book: Know All Your Options and Choose the Method That Is Right for You* (Avon, MA: Adams Media, 2004).

Leavitt, Judith Walzer. *Make Room for Daddy: The Journey from Waiting Room to Birthing Room* (Chapel Hill, NC: University of North Carolina Press, 2010).

ORGANIZATIONS

American College of Nurse-Midwives
8403 Colesville Road, Suite 1550
Silver Spring, MD 20910
240-485-1800
www.midwife.org

The American Congress of Obstetricians and Gynecologists
PO Box 96920
Washington, DC 20090-6920
202-638-5577
www.acog.org

Lamaze International
2025 M Street, NW Suite 800
Washington, DC 20036
800-368-4404
www.lamaze.org

Midwives Alliance of North America
611 Pennsylvania Ave., SE, #1700
Washington, DC 20003
888-923-6262
www.mana.org

Conception/Fertility

BOOKS

Weschler, Toni. *Taking Charge of Your Fertility: The Definitive Guide to Natural Birth Control, Pregnancy Achievement, and Reproductive Health* (New York: Collins, 2006).

ORGANIZATIONS

American Society for Reproductive Medicine (ASRM)
Formerly the American Fertility Society
1209 Montgomery Hwy.
Birmingham, Al 35216-2809
205-978-5000
www.asrm.org

RESOLVE: The National Infertility Association
1760 Old Meadow Road, Suite 500
McLean, VA 22102
703-556-7172
www.resolve.org

Cooking and Nutrition

BOOKS

Gruber, John, and Chris Potter. *My Wife Doesn't Cook: A Survival Guide for Men* (Gruber-Potter, 1998).

Hensperger, Beth, and Julie Kaufmann. *Not Your Mother's Slow Cooker Cookbook* (Boston, MA: Harvard Common Press, 2005).

Ray, Rachael. *Rachael Ray's Look + Cook* (New York: Clarkson Potter, 2010).

Robinson, Claire. *5 Ingredient Fix: Easy, Elegant, and Irresistible Recipes* (New York: Grand Central Life & Style, 2010).

Especially for Dads

BOOKS

Nelson, Kevin. *The Everything® Father-to-Be Book: A Survival Guide for Men* (Avon, MA: Adams Media, 2003).

WEBSITES

Babycenter.com
www.babycenter.com
A resource for new expectant parents that includes message boards just for dads.

Financial Planning, Wills, and Insurance

BOOKS

American Bar Association. *The American Bar Association Guide to Wills and Estates: Everything You Need to Know About Wills, Estates, Trusts and Taxes, 3rd Ed* (New York: Random House Reference, 2009).

Caverly, N. Brian, and Jordan Simon. *Estate Planning for Dummies* (New York: Hungry Minds, 2003).

Fowles, Debby. *The Everything® Personal Finance in Your 20s and 30s Book, 2nd Edition: Erase Your Debt, Personalize Your Budget, and Plan Now to Secure Your Future* (Avon, MA: Adams Media, 2008).

COMPUTER SOFTWARE

Quicken Willmaker Plus (Nolo Press, 2011).

WEBSITES

DoYourOwnWill.com
www.doyourownwill.com
A site that enables you to create a simple will online.

Life Quotes, Inc.
www.lifequotes.com
A source for insurance quotes from a number of major companies.

Making-a-legal-will.com
www.making-a-legal-will.com
A site linking you to forms and services that can help you in
writing a will.

Saving for College.com
www.savingforcollege.com
Information on 529 plans and many other aspects of paying for
a college education.

Multiple Births

BOOKS

Leiter, Gila. *Everything You Need to Know to Have a Healthy Twin
Pregnancy* (New York: Dell, 2000).
Luke, Barbara, and Tamara Eberlein. *When You're Expecting Twins,
Triplets, or Quads: Proven Guidelines for a Healthy Multiple
Pregnancy*, 3rd ed. (New York: Perennial, 2010).

ORGANIZATIONS

Triplet Connection
P.O. Box 429
Spring City, Utah 84662
435-851-1105
www.tripletconnection.org

Pampering and Gift Items

WEBSITES

Zingerman's
www.Zingermans.com
A site with a variety of food gifts to order for your wife.

Florists Transworld Delivery (FTD)
www.ftd.com
Sending flowers to her office from time to time will cause her
coworkers to remind her what a good guy you are, no matter
what she thinks.

Vermont Teddy Bear Company
www.vermontteddybear.com
A site that sells fancy teddy bears, including a number of "new
baby" bears and a pregnant bear.

Shopping.com
www.shopping.com
A site that offers a vast selection of gifts for the new mom, like
charms and name bracelets.

Goldspeed.com
www.goldspeed.com
This site sells a cameo of a newborn with its mother—a good
"push gift."

Baby Heirlooms
www.babyheirlooms.com
Sells upscale gifts for the new baby.

Paternity Leave

ORGANIZATIONS

Families and Work Institute
267 Fifth Avenue, 2nd Floor
New York, NY 10016
212-465-2044
www.familiesandwork.org

National Partnership for Women & Families
1875 Connecticut Avenue, NW, Suite 650
Washington, DC 20009
202-986-2600
www.nationalpartnership.org

U.S. Department of Labor
Wage and Hour Division
866-487-9243 (toll-free helpline)
www.dol.gov/WHD

Postpartum Depression

BOOKS

Dalton, Katharina, with Wendy Holton. *Depression After
    Childbirth: How to Recognize, Treat, and Prevent Postnatal
    Depression* (New York: Oxford University Press, 2001).

ORGANIZATIONS

Postpartum Education for Parents
www.sbpep.org

Baby Safety

WEBSITES

U.S. Consumer Product Safety Commission
www.cpsc.gov
Offers the latest in child safety information and lists products
    that have been recalled.

KidSource OnLine
www.kidsource.com
Provides the basic rules of safety from newborn through
    childhood.
Safe & Secure Baby
www.safeandsecurebaby.com

The one-stop shop for your babyproofing needs.

Second-Time Fathers

BOOKS

Leonard, Joan. *Twice Blessed: Everything You Need to Know About Having a Second Child—Preparing Yourself, Your Marriage, and Your Firstborn for a New Family of Four* (New York: St. Martin's Griffin, 2000).

Stay-at-Home Fathering

WEBSITES

Dad Stays Home.com
www.dadstayshome.com
Offers the stay-at-home dad a much-needed forum for support. It also boasts an Internet resource link to various other sites.

Index

When You Don't Have Time for Anything Else

Visit our Cereal for Supper blog and join other over-inundated, under-celebrated, multi-tasking moms for an (almost) daily allowance of parenting advice—and absolution.

You won't learn how to make handmade Martha Stewart–inspired hankie holders or elaborate gourmet dinners—but you will find heaping spoonfuls of support and a few laughs along the way!

Sign up for our newsletter now at
www.adamsmedia.com/blog/parenting
And get our FREE Top Ten Recipes for Picky Eaters!